O9-BTO-131

Praise for *Cahokia*

"A compellingly argued and highly engaging account of a lost civilization in America's own backyard. This is a story that ultimately deserves to be better known, even if we think we already know it."   —*Chicago Tribune*

"In *Cahokia*, Timothy R. Pauketat tells the story of the mounds, from what archeologists have been able to discover about their origins nearly a thousand years ago to their near destruction and partially successful preservation in the modern age."
        —*The Wall Street Journal*

"Pauketat's work has added a new veneer of glamour to good old Cahokia."   —*Riverfront Times*

"Illuminating . . . Page by page, Pauketat compiles the fascinating details of a complex archaeological puzzle . . . invites opposing viewpoints, and his writing is rich in you-are-there detail, making this an archaeological adventure suitable for pre-Columbian enthusiasts as well as inquisitive laymen."
        —*Publishers Weekly* (starred review)

"Pauketat utilizes the latest revelations uncovered by historians and archaeologists to write a compact but thorough survey of this powerful but enigmatic culture . . . provocative . . . this is an interesting and informative explanation of a fascinating but still puzzling civilization."   —*Booklist*

"Absorbing . . . A happy marriage of professional scholarship and childlike enthusiasm."   —*Kirkus Reviews*

ABOUT THE AUTHOR

Timothy R. Pauketat is a professor of anthropology at the University of Illinois, Urbana-Champaign. His books include *Chiefdoms and Other Archaeological Delusions* and *Ancient Cahokia and the Mississippians*. He lives in Illinois.

OTHER TITLES
IN THE PENGUIN LIBRARY
OF AMERICAN INDIAN HISTORY

The Cherokee Nation and the Trail of Tears
Theda Purdue and Michael D. Green

The Shawnees and the War for America
Colin G. Calloway

American Indians and the Law
N. Bruce Duthu

Iroquois Diplomacy on the Early American Frontier
Timothy J. Shannon

The Lakotas and the Black Hills
Jeff Ostler

Ojibwe Women and the Survival of Indian Community
Brenda J. Child

GENERAL EDITOR: Colin G. Calloway

ADVISORY BOARD:
Brenda J. Child, Philip J. Deloria, Frederick E. Hoxie

CAHOKIA

Ancient America's Great City

on the Mississippi

TIMOTHY R. PAUKETAT

THE PENGUIN LIBRARY
OF AMERICAN INDIAN HISTORY

PENGUIN BOOKS

PENGUIN BOOKS

Published by the Penguin Group
Penguin Group (USA) Inc., 375 Hudson Street, New York, New York 10014, U.S.A.
Penguin Group (Canada), 90 Eglinton Avenue East, Suite 700, Toronto,
Ontario, Canada M4P 2Y3 (a division of Pearson Penguin Canada Inc.)
Penguin Books Ltd, 80 Strand, London WC2R 0RL, England
Penguin Ireland, 25 St Stephen's Green, Dublin 2, Ireland (a division of Penguin Books Ltd)
Penguin Group (Australia), 250 Camberwell Road, Camberwell,
Victoria 3124, Australia (a division of Pearson Australia Group Pty Ltd)
Penguin Books India Pvt Ltd, 11 Community Centre, Panchsheel Park, New Delhi – 110 017, India
Penguin Group (NZ), 67 Apollo Drive, Rosedale, North Shore 0632,
New Zealand (a division of Pearson New Zealand Ltd)
Penguin Books (South Africa) (Pty) Ltd, 24 Sturdee Avenue,
Rosebank, Johannesburg 2196, South Africa

Penguin Books Ltd, Registered Offices: 80 Strand, London WC2R 0RL, England

First published in the United States of America by Viking Penguin,
a member of Penguin Group (USA) Inc. 2009
Published in Penguin Books 2010

5   7   9   10   8   6

Copyright © Timothy R. Pauketat, 2009
All rights reserved

Image on page 30 used by permission of Cahokia Mounds State Historic Site. Painting by Paul Bradford.

THE LIBRARY OF CONGRESS HAS CATALOGED THE HARDCOVER EDITION AS FOLLOWS:
Pauketat, Timothy R.
Cahokia : ancient America's great city on the Mississippi / Timothy R. Pauketat.
p.   cm.— (The Penguin library of American Indian history)
Includes bibliographical references and index.
ISBN 978-0-670-02090-4 (hc.)
ISBN 978-0-14-311747-6 (pbk.)
1. Cahokia Mounds State Historic Park (Ill.)   2. Indians of North America—Illinois—Cahokia Mounds
State Historic Park—Antiquities.   3. Mississippian culture—Illinois—American Bottom.   4. Mississippian
culture—Middle West.   5. American Bottom (Ill.)—Antiquities.   6. Illinois—Antiquities.   7. Middle
West—Antiquities.   8. Excavations (Archaeology)—Illinois—American Bottom.   I. Title.
E99.M6815P375 2009
977.3'86—dc22   2008054092

Printed in the United States of America
Set in Granjon   Designed by Katy Riegal

Except in the United States of America, this book is sold subject to the condition
that it shall not, by way of trade or otherwise, be lent, resold, hired out, or otherwise
circulated without the publisher's prior consent in any form of binding or cover other
than that in which it is published and without a similar condition including
this condition being imposed on the subsequent purchaser.

The scanning, uploading and distribution of this book via the Internet or via any other means
without the permission of the publisher is illegal and punishable by law. Please purchase only
authorized electronic editions, and do not participate in or encourage electronic piracy
of copyrighted materials. Your support of the author's rights is appreciated.

*In memory
of Mike, Preston, Harriet, Warren,
Al, and Chuck*

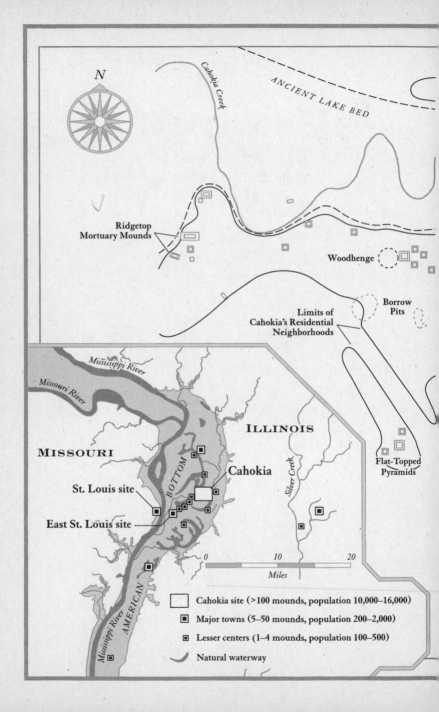

N

Cahokia Creek

ANCIENT LAKE BED

Ridgetop Mortuary Mounds

Woodhenge

Limits of Cahokia's Residential Neighborhoods

Borrow Pits

Mississippi River

Missouri River

ILLINOIS

MISSOURI

BOTTOM

Cahokia

Silver Creek

St. Louis site

East St. Louis site

Flat-Topped Pyramids

```
0          10          20
        Miles
```

Mississippi River

AMERICAN

◻ Cahokia site (>100 mounds, population 10,000–16,000)

▣ Major towns (5–50 mounds, population 200–2,000)

▣ Lesser centers (1–4 mounds, population 100–500)

〰 Natural waterway

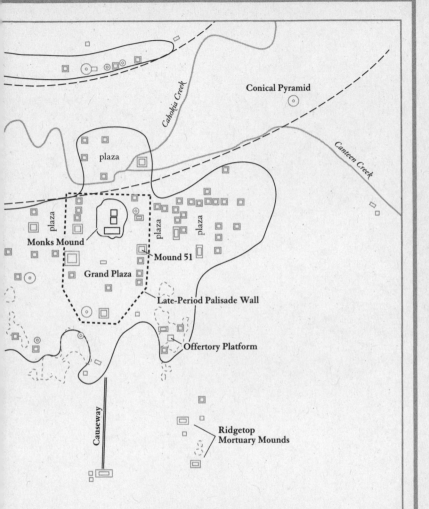

Conical Pyramid

Cahokia Creek

Canteen Creek

plaza

plaza

Monks Mound

plaza

plaza

Mound 51

Grand Plaza

Late-Period Palisade Wall

Offertory Platform

Causeway

Ridgetop
Mortuary Mounds

MAP OF THE
ANCIENT CITY OF CAHOKIA

0   500   1000

Yards

© 2009 Jeffrey L. Ward

CONTENTS

1

THE MOTHER OF NATIVE NORTH AMERICA

1

2

SUPERNOVA

11

3

WALKING INTO CAHOKIA

25

4

THE ORIGINAL ROLLING STONES

36

5

GHOSTS OF ARCHAEOLOGISTS

51

6

DISCOVERY AT MOUND 72

69

7

TWIN HEROES

85

8

AMERICAN INDIAN ROYALTY

99

9

DIGGING FOR THE GODDESS

119

10

WRESTLING WITH THE GODS

136

11

TREASURE MAPS OF THE PAST
151

12

HIGH PLAINS DRIFTING
161

Acknowledgments
171

Notes
175

Index
187

1

THE MOTHER OF NATIVE NORTH AMERICA

IN THE EARLY HOURS before sunrise, for part of each year, the planet Venus shines as a "morning star." Slowly it disappears as the rising sun turns darkness to sky blue. To the ancient Maya and others, this Morning Star was a god, the "Sun-Carrier," created to transport the sun into the world of people. In ancient North America, it was viewed as a masculine deity who—at a key moment in history—assumed human form. When seen later in the year as the Evening Star, Venus was considered a feminine god. She appeared then with the setting sun, a harbinger of the night and the netherworld beyond the horizon. Sometimes seen as a creator goddess, she also took human form and, in the flesh, made history.

A thousand years ago, the Morning and Evening stars were central players in an American Indian drama, characters at once mythic—sky gods with supernatural powers—and human, driven by violence, politics, and religion. And this drama was at the heart of a place we now call Cahokia, ancient America's one true city

north of Mexico—as large in its day as London—and the political
capital of a most unusual Indian nation.

At that time all the stars and planets in the Northern Hemisphere's night sky were visible above Cahokia, situated in a broad
expanse of Mississippi River bottomland just east of what is now St.
Louis, Missouri. Cahokia's people looked to the Morning and Evening stars for guidance and—inspired by ideas from Mesoamerica,
possibly brought back from Cahokian rulers' travels or priests' vision
quests—incorporated them into a religion that would displace traditions across the American Midwest, South, and Plains.[1]

Nowadays, one can barely see the stars at night from St. Louis.
Tall buildings crowd the sky, and streetlights blot out the stars even
as the growth of modern civilization erases the archaeological remains of the ancient North Americans. Still, Cahokia sits silently,
awaiting the almost three hundred thousand visitors who come to
the site each year. Taking in its grass-covered mounds, vast open
spaces, and large watery borrow pits, they ponder the lives of the
original inhabitants of North America's largest pyramidal-mound
complex, centered by what is, in fact, the third-largest pyramid in
the entire New World.

At one time, there were more than two hundred packed-earth
pyramids, or "mounds," at Cahokia and its suburbs. More than half
of these were built in a five-square-mile zone that was designed
with reference to the four sacred directions and the upper and lower
worlds. The pyramids were arranged around vast open plazas and
were surrounded, in turn, by thousands of pole-and-thatch houses,
temples, and public buildings. At its height, Cahokia had a population in excess of ten thousand, with at least twenty or thirty thousand more in the outlying towns and farming settlements that
ranged for fifty miles in every direction.

From the beginnings of the Euroamerican city of St. Louis,
some of the biggest and most important ancient American monuments were leveled to make way for new developments. Twenty-

five mounds were destroyed in St. Louis before the Civil War. Forty-five more were taken down across the river in East St. Louis shortly thereafter. Scores were lost in Cahokia proper, including the second largest, removed by steam shovel in 1930.

In the 1800s, most people knew that the ancient earthen mounds being destroyed were the works of human hands, but surprisingly few suspected that they had been built by American Indians. Some believed that a lost race of civilized non-Indian Mound Builders had constructed these impressive tumuli, like those all along the American frontier west of the Alleghany Mountains, down the Ohio valley, and dotting the Mississippi trench. These mysterious Mound Builders, they thought, must have been wiped out by the later, warlike American Indians, or perhaps they migrated to Mexico to found the great civilizations of the Aztec and Maya.

What remains of Cahokia's 3,200 acres of great pyramids, spacious plazas, thatched-roof temples, houses, astronomical observatories, and planned neighborhoods suffers from deterioration. The core of the site is preserved within a state park. The rest is wedged between modern highways or buried beneath factories and houses in the greater St. Louis metropolitan area. Much has been lost. Perhaps this is why few people—even few archaeologists—have a full sense of this American Indian city and its place in world history.

Although a complete picture of ancient Cahokia may never be possible, archaeologists continue to study, make discoveries, and reinterpret what is known about the city and its influence on surrounding areas and future generations. Their findings call into question some long-held beliefs—for instance, that ecologically sensitive, peaceful, mystical, and egalitarian peoples freely roamed the North American continent, never overpopulating or overexploiting their environments; or that these peoples were not subject to such base human emotions as avarice, greed, and covetousness and thus could not have built cities or allowed power to be concentrated in the hands of elites.

What is exciting about the archaeological discoveries at Cahokia is that they point to an alternative interpretation: that a "big bang" occurred there in which an abrupt burst of large-scale construction created an unprecedented American Indian city. What does this "big bang" mean? It means that political and social change happened here quickly, effected by visionaries who shaped events and influenced a group of people in a profound way, and that this influence spread to other areas at that time and to later cultures. Underlying this interpretation is the idea that all people everywhere actively make history. The lives of all the people of the past and all those living shape the larger world. Even choosing inaction has historical implications. Civilizations can rise and fall, to adapt Margaret Mead's famous quotation, as a result of the actions of a small group of people combined with the inaction of many others. Making sense of these actions and inactions can be a difficult task for archaeologists, who must distinguish between how people lived and how they wanted to be perceived as living. Cahokia's big bang is a case study in how people can combine to create great historical change.

Cahokia may be a powerful example of such a process, but there are others. Take, for example, the case of Spiro, Oklahoma. In 1933, a group of men formed a company to loot the large mounds of this pre-Columbian town in what remains a sparsely populated patch near the Oklahoma-Arkansas border. They found what a later archaeologist dubbed the "Great Mortuary," the richest single deposit of burial goods ever unearthed in the United States. At the time, a reporter for the *Kansas City Star* called it "A 'King Tut' Tomb in the Arkansas Valley."[2] Given the great hoard of cultural objects buried there, it seemed likely that a powerful pharaoh and a great population must have lived in the rural Arkansas River valley ages ago.

It made for quite a news story, but it wasn't the whole truth. Decades later, advanced ground-penetrating radar and several ar-

chaeological excavations revealed that the site was never very populous. Moreover, careful study of the burials led archaeologists to
conclude that there were no powerful rulers among them. Instead,
the hoard of objects in the Great Mortuary vastly overstated the
actual power and influence of the community's leading families.
Perhaps they were attempting to convince a more dubious public
of their stature. The Spiro treasure, it turned out, was a composite of
wonderful things from the across the Midwest and South that had
been collected by the high-ranking Spiroans. Probably proficient
traders but not strong rulers, they created something in death that
their dead never had much of in life: the appearance of political
power.[3]

Whatever effects this lavish burial of wealth with the dead had
at the time, it certainly seems to have fooled the twentieth-century
newspaper reporters. While disappointing to some, the real story
was hardly a surprise to archaeologists. To some extent, all civilizations are built on projections, propaganda, and half-truths—
measures undertaken to create for posterity a stature or reputation
that may not match reality. Even King Tut's entombed wealth wasn't
all his.

A second good example of how the ancient storytelling of
would-be elites might be misread in the present can be found in Mexico, at the Zapotec city of Monte Albán, built on a mountaintop
overlooking today's Oaxaca City. At one time, Monte Albán was
assumed to have been the crowning achievement of a people aspir-
ing to create a better society for all. A series of stone carvings of
oddly positioned human forms was thought by early archaeologists
to depict individual dancers, the so-called Danzantes.[4] However, as
it turned out, that story also ran headlong into archaeological fact.
Later archaeologists digging into the city's ruins and searching
among the remains of abandoned outlying settlements found evidence that Monte Albán was built from scratch at a time of rapid
political change in the Valley of Oaxaca, around 500 BC—the valley

experienced its own big bang, in other words. Archaeologists now realize that Monte Albán's rulers ritually killed captive enemy leaders, commemorating their mutilated bodies as the Danzantes, in order to impress the local farmers, who would visit the city periodically for community ceremonies.

As these stories suggest, archaeologists must take great care in interpreting the clues left behind by ancient societies, or they may end up being fooled by misleading evidence of a great or noble history. In fact, as will become clear, part of the challenge of figuring out the story of Cahokia involves transcending the biases of mostly male storytellers. Such "official histories"—most often seen in archaeology in the artwork and iconography produced under the aegis of politicians—are always written or sponsored by those who ruled. They give viewers, at best, half of the truth.

The other half consists of "unofficial histories," the unsung and uncelebrated narratives of the defeated and the powerless. These are typically expressed in the many ways in which people did or did not conform to, accept, or accommodate such storytelling. Such alternative truths might have been disguised or hidden from the watchful eyes of the officials by necessity. But if archaeologists look closely, they can find these unofficial histories, which present a different picture of the rise of civilization in ancient North America.

A thousand years ago, there really was a big bang in the middle of the Mississippi River valley. Around the year 1050 (AD or CE),[5] social life, political organization, religious belief, art, and culture were radically transformed. At the epicenter of events was a radical new kind of social and political experiment: a planned capital city built around a big idea, one of such magnitude and force that it impelled tens of thousands of people to drop what they were doing and follow a new path.

What was the big idea, and who were its advocates? Was there a Cahokian leader—an aggressive autocrat, warlord, or foreigner—who grabbed power and coerced people to conform? Did a clever politician or altruistic clan leader happen upon an opportunity to unify—through marriage, political alliance, or ceremony—a number of formerly autonomous families, clans, or whole settlements? Perhaps a charismatic priest had a vision like those known to the indigenous prophets of the later historical era[6] or was inspired by things he had seen in distant lands to the south, perhaps in Mexico. There are strong suggestions that the Cahokians, in building their vision into the landscape, drew on Mesoamerican models. Their possible descendants or those of their allies or enemies practiced Mesoamerican-style human sacrifice, incorporated obelisklike posts into their worship, relayed stories of superhuman men and women who wore distinctive garments and ear ornaments, used Mesoamerican-type flint daggers, and understood the cosmos in ways occasionally parallel to Mesoamerican notions.

Certainly, someone or some governing body designed a city from scratch at Cahokia. The leaders superimposed a new plan directly over the spaces, houses, and traditions of an old village. And then they established governmental controls over peoples living in all directions—an unprecedented move in the history of ancient America north of Mexico.

But governments don't rise and fall every day. And they don't come about without the help of thousands of followers, the people who would have done the actual building of the great pyramids of earth, the flat, open plazas, and the huge wooden buildings. This would be especially true of a growing population of people who were used to living without a regionally centralized government.

Thus, for Cahokia's new government to work, some people must have accommodated it or been coerced by it. And since the latter is a costly short-term tactic, civilizations are almost always built on the formation of consensus or on ideologies that legitimize the rule of a few in the minds of the many. So when archaeologists talk about the rise of ancient states, they are typically talking about the emergence of a whole way of life or a new ritual-religious order and not just a government. How did the Cahokians obtain the co-operation of tens of thousands of people?

The effects of events at Cahokia around 1050 were immediate, abrupt, and long-lasting across the entire midcontinent. The people of this North American city seem to have created their own culture, then proceeded to spread it across the Midwest and into the South and Plains with a religious fervor—and with effects some archaeologists have compared to those of the Olmec and Chavín "mother cultures" of Mexico and Peru. Another theory is that Cahokia's culture was directly inspired by such Latin American archetypes, with the Cahokian gods and supernatural beliefs possibly being borrowed from Mexican religions. Whatever the case, all archaeologists refer to the North American variety as the Mississippian culture or civilization, named after the river along which sit most of its known sites. Like the Latin American varieties, Mississippian culture was based on beliefs about ancestors, the stars, maize agriculture, and powerful male and female superhuman characters. And it was continuously reinvented and adapted to fit local conditions.

Some of the culture's facets displayed surprising longevity. When the Spanish and French arrived in the sixteenth and seventeenth centuries, they documented the descendants of the Mississippians as practicing maize-based agriculture, living in populous towns, playing a distinctive team sport, producing unique forms of pottery, and observing religions centered on earth and sky gods, including the Morning and Evening stars. Such practices link the later Mississippians to the founders of Cahokia and the central ideas of the earliest phases of Mississippian civilization. They also link, in other ways, ancient northern North America to Mexico. And they connect the history of the United States to the greater history of pre-Columbian America. The links are tangible, witnessed by rock-art maps, excavated art objects and gaming stones, and the legends of American Indians, and buried in the mortuary tombs of the early

Cahokians. This book follows the hard evidence to arrive back at the beginning.

Today's archaeologists see the spread of Cahokia's influence in the shapes of platform mounds and ancestral temples, in the works of art buried with the dead across the Midwest and South, in the marine-shell beads traded to distant lands, and among the pottery shards decorated with Cahokian insignia scattered on the floors of Indian homes from Wisconsin and Minnesota in the north to Oklahoma and Louisiana in the south. Some places seem to have been colonial outposts or missions where traveling Cahokians might have sought to convert locals. The most obvious of these are found about four hundred miles north of Cahokia in the rugged lands of southern Wisconsin. They include large settlements occupied by southerners, probably Cahokians, who built flat-topped mounds, carried Cahokian pots and tools northward, and practiced a Cahokian religion.[7] At other sites locals appear to have enthusiastically copied that which they considered to be Cahokian. Distant people—perhaps from as far away as New York and Florida in the east, New Mexico in the west, and Mexico in the south—may have heard reports of this new city of black-earth pyramids, red cedar walls, cypress uprights, yellow thatched roofs, and fragrantly burning tobacco along the Mississippi River in the heart of North America. Many went to see what it was all about.

So Cahokia's transformation, like the big bang that created the universe, involved more than just the building of a new capital city. Cahokia, some archaeologists now believe, offered much to its inhabitants and neighbors: peace, religion, food, friends, allies, order, and security. From the archaeological evidence, surrounding peoples were eager to join in the new social experiment, making this expansion a kind of great civilizing social movement, with almost cultlike effects. At sites near Cahokia, mixed in with Cahokian ceremonial debris or discovered inside houses, archaeologists have found the unusual pottery and tools of immigrants from what are now Indiana, Missouri, and Arkansas. Occasionally, they also find objects made in Louisiana, South Dakota, or Oklahoma. Apparently, people living in parts of the Mississippi, Ohio, and Missouri river valleys visited Cahokia and took part in what must have seemed a native renaissance centered in the ancient American heartland. That is not to say that everyone joined so readily. There was a darker side to Cahokia's expansion: Some might have experienced it as an unstoppable new threat.

In any case, the big bang of the North American interior, like its better-known counterpart in astrophysics, was the beginning of a new universe, a turning point in history. It reset the historical clocks that had seen generations of rising and setting suns, moons, and Morning and Evening stars. It disrupted the histories of the unsuspecting people of the woodlands and plains of eastern North America. It ushered in a whole new way of life across much of the North American continent. Civilization's switch had been flipped on, and a single brilliant light instantly shone across the Midwest, South, and eastern Plains.

2

SUPERNOVA

BY THE MIDDLE of the eleventh century, rival European kingdoms and principalities were emerging from the cultural and economic Dark Ages of the post-Roman world. The climate was warming as much as a few degrees Fahrenheit in the Northern Hemisphere, allowing Inuit hunters in North America's Arctic to move east and Leif Eriksson's Norse men and women to sail west, colonizing both Greenland and Newfoundland within a few decades.

Descendants of Viking lords still ruled some northern European cities outside Scandinavia: Dublin, York, Moscow, Kiev. They traded with the Islamic peoples in southwest Asia, with Christians in Central Europe, and with Arabs in North Africa. Scores of small medieval kingdoms, trading city-states, and emirates dotted sub-Saharan Africa, the Near East, and India, also connected in part by trade. The Chola empire dominated southern India's cities while, farther east, Angkor Wat sat at the heart of the Khmer realm in present-day Cambodia. To the north was China, the superpower of the medieval world, where astrologers of the Song dynasty's emperor, who ruled millions from the capital at Kaifeng, watched the night skies.

In the New World, South America's Andean backbone was segmented into a series of small territorial states that remained after the collapse of the large Wari and Tiwanaku states in modern-day Peru. Here, during the Late Intermediate period, walled towns and hilltop-refuge sites attest to a fragmented political landscape. Mesoamerica, too—the peoples, places, and cultures of southern Mexico, Guatemala, Belize, and Honduras—was mostly carved up into small territorial states. The great Zapotec center at Monte Albán was but a memory by the eleventh century, a ghostly mountaintop used for royal tombs. So, too, was the empire of the great Classic period city of Teotihuacán, which had been sacked and then abandoned after 700.

Other Mexican cities, called Post-Classic because they didn't quite match the greatness of Teotihuacán, had emerged to fill the imperial vacuum. By the mid-eleventh century, these included El Tajín, Xochicalco, and Tula. A pan-Mesoamerican "Toltec horizon"—perhaps centered at Tula, just north of today's Mexico City—extended into the Yucatán Peninsula, most evident at the ancient behemoth of Chichén Itzá. Everywhere, these Post-Classic people attempted to re-create Teotihuacán. The old rain and feathered-serpent gods of Teotihuacán reappeared in other forms far and wide. For instance, far to the north, in the Mimbres valley in what is now southern New Mexico, agricultural people during the eleventh century engaged in elaborate rituals involving black-painted white pots; on some, the artist-potters painted the Teotihuacán rain god, known to the Aztec centuries later as Tlaloc and to the Maya as Chac.

The rituals and pots of the Mimbres valley, however, were less elaborate than those of the mysteriously remote Chaco Canyon of northwestern New Mexico. During the tenth through the twelfth centuries at Chaco, powerful leaders unified local farmers, immigrants, and pilgrims through the great public constructions of a dozen multistoried Great Houses. The entire canyon was a political-ritual amphitheater, with audiences of believers and pilgrims standing on the canyon's rim looking down on the Great Houses and up to the sun, the moon, and the stars.

Meanwhile, in the middle of the Mississippi River valley, the warmer years leading up to the mid-eleventh century had nurtured the development of a prosperous society of corn-growing villages near present-day St. Louis. Most were modest, sometimes just a few huts around an open courtyard no bigger than a Little League baseball diamond. In the middle of each courtyard was a single vertical post some four to eight inches in diameter—a marker of group identity, perhaps even a representation of an important ancestor.

Centuries later, an English colonist on the East Coast depicted horticultural villagers—often called "Woodland Indians" by anthropologists—dancing around a circle of upright posts, each carved with a human face. Similarly, as recorded by anthropologists, Plains Indians revered certain posts or circles of posts as symbols of the ancestors, representations of the Milky Way, and access points to the sun, the stars, and the gods. Some people even climbed such posts to reenact the journeys that they believed the ghosts of dead relatives would make across the Path of Souls, or the Milky Way. Others, including the descendants of Mississippi valley people, kept their sacred poles in special buildings. The Omaha, for instance, referred to theirs as the Venerable Man, praying and making offerings to him.

With such an important marker post, the courtyard was special and unified the families who identified with one another. These families got together to build their houses, which were intended as sleeping shelters for individual nuclear households. They did this by first carefully digging a neat rectangular pit almost twice as long as a person's body length and one body-length wide. Then they built the framework by planting the ends of good-sized saplings in rows of individually dug post holes along the edges of the house pit. The wispy long ends of the saplings, which were stripped of their bark, would then have been pulled together and tied to form an arbor-shaped roof before being covered with thatch or woven mats.

The population of this region, which would come to be the center of the great Cahokian city, could not have been large in the tenth and early eleventh centuries. Based on numbers of known villages and surrounding smaller hamlets, perhaps as many as a few thousand people lived in a twenty-five-hundred-square-mile area. Each self-governing village or group of allied villages needed open farm fields, garden spaces, and hunting territory; they could not have been packed too densely together into any stretch of Mississippi floodplain or hilly uplands without running the risk of conflicts over land or perceived infringements erupting between families. Daily life in the warm season was centered on tending crops and processing food for one's family or for stockpiling winter stores. The cold season doubtless witnessed hunting forays into the interior woodlands or prairie lands of Illinois and Missouri.

Over the course of a year, political and religious leaders probably hosted community festivals tied to the ritual calendar and to the growing season; planting would commence as the sun moved ever higher in the sky and the springtime thunderstorms arrived in April. Religious rituals at such annual festivals honored the gods and the village ancestors, whose bones or sacred objects were kept in the temples—elaborate pole-and-thatch versions of houses—at the largest settlements. Group councils probably met in square buildings some three to four times the size of an ordinary house. At various sites in the region, archaeologists have excavated the foundations of such public buildings, sometimes with floors covering around 325 square feet, the size of a large room in a modern American home. Along the sides of some of these council houses, there is evidence of enough seating for two or three dozen people.

It is likely that the people who met for such councils were representatives of neighboring villages. They would negotiate access to common resources, resolve disputes, mark important life events, and mourn the passing of previous generations. Having traveled from locations several hours to several days away, the visitors might spend the night and share a meal with their hosts. Indeed, among the broken pot shards in excavated village garbage pits, archaeologists have found indications of pottery from other villages in the region and beyond, identifiable based on the distinctive clays used to make them. In other words, while villages might have governed themselves, they were not socially isolated or culturally insular. There was regular interchange between them. There might even have been large-scale feasts or huge ceremonial events hosted by some prominent families from the largest villages that drew up to hundreds of visitors from the surrounding area.

In this way, the initial steps toward a big bang had already been taken in the decades leading up to 1050. By that point, certain agricultural villages occupying elevated ridges on blufftops along the Mississippi floodplain had grown large and consisted of several courtyard groups strung together on a hill or prominent ridge. The families at some of these villages were probably influential, as they lived in slightly larger houses and had more stored food at their disposal. At the two or three largest villages, there were up to several small, four-sided earthen pyramids, each of which was surmounted by a community temple.

The most prominent members of the community lived at the largest of the villages, one of which was the original Cahokia. By the early eleventh century, "Old Cahokia" was home to more than a thousand people. This made it the largest village in this stretch of riverine heartland at the center of ancient America's Corn Belt. It was like a small town made up of neighborhoods, each comprising a series of adjacent houses with their own courtyards, perhaps all arranged around some larger open public space in the middle.

Like a handful of other large villages, Old Cahokia may have been a seat of community government. But if it was—and that's a point debated by archaeologists—then its government remained local and ceremonial, a minor confederacy of farming villages. Then again, by this time, people had already begun relocating to Old Cahokia from smaller, less successful villages in the surrounding region. They probably spoke the same language and had the same basic customs as the Old Cahokians.

But other immigrants also moved to Old Cahokia from farther afield, as far away as present-day southern Missouri. By looking at the broken pottery in the kitchen garbage at Old Cahokia, we can see that some of the potters had learned their craft, and probably their cooking habits, south and west of the confluence of the Ohio and Mississippi rivers. Such potters and their families might not have spoken the same dialect or practiced the same traditions as the Old Cahokians. Their foreign cuisine, speech patterns, cultural practices, and physical appearance were probably easy to spot and possibly, for parochial locals, a source of awe and mystery. For this reason, the most influential families of the floodplain might well have sought to acquire this exotic aura by marrying into foreign families and bringing their unusual spouses to live with them at Old Cahokia.

Some of the foreigners might have been elites with reputations established in far-off lands. Cahokia was not the first ceremonial center to have been constructed in eastern North America, nor was it the first to incorporate giant earthen mounds as a critical architectural feature. There were great mound-building episodes going back beyond 3500 BCE in what is today northeastern Louisiana. Indeed, the oldest pyramids in the New World, we now know, were built not in Mexico or Peru but astride the bayous and backwaters of the lower Mississippi River. One of the earliest settled towns in the New World, featuring one of the largest earthen mounds ever built in North America, was the unprecedented center of Poverty Point, in northeastern Louisiana. There, residents hosted great public events and converted exotic raw materials (flints, soap stone, paint stones, and crystals) into religious icons as early as 1600 BCE.

Lumped together by explorers and early scholars as the Mound Builders, ancient indigenous peoples across the Midwest and South ceremoniously piled up earth here and there for various reasons until the European invasion and the decimation of the continent's indigenous population. Archaeologists have long recognized a series of mound-building traditions, most famously including the Middle Woodland Scioto or Hopewell people of Ohio and their contemporaries in Louisiana and Illinois around and after the time of Christ. There's also the Effigy Mound Culture of southern Wisconsin and neighboring portions of other states, where the Late Woodlands peoples, descended from earlier Hopewell-like peoples, interred their dead in or near modest tumuli built to look like thunderbirds, underwater spirits, panthers, and bears. Like the earlier Woodland peoples, they predate the well-known Mississippian cultures that covered North America's midlands and southlands after the rise and fall of Cahokia.

None of these "traditions" were self-perpetuating, and great gaps exist in the historical records of various regions where very little earthen construction occurred or where people migrated from here to there.[1] The lower Mississippi valley—Arkansas, Louisiana, Mississippi—witnessed the closest thing to cultural continuity that we know of in pre-Columbian North America. There, each generation of people down through the centuries seemed to have looked back to the past and revisited or rebuilt the mounded places all

around them, effectively reinventing tradition time after time with
their own earthen constructions.² Some were for burial, and others
were platforms or stages for community performances.

It seems unlikely that any of these early mound centers was occupied by more than a few hundred people at any point in its history.
Some were entirely vacant for long periods, serving as pilgrimage
sites or ceremonial centers where people might go to commune with
ancient spirits or otherworldly powers. Others were focal points
for sedentary communities that were otherwise dispersed across the
wider landscape. Such dispersed communities made sense, since
many people throughout eastern North America still moved about to
gather wild foods in addition to tending garden crops. Agricultural
intensification—especially the focus on maize or corn—didn't begin
in earnest until the eighth century CE or so, and even then it was
spotty.

However, after 800, lower midwestern and midsouthern peoples were taking the initial steps toward intensifying agricultural
production. Villages of people doing the more intense food production along the Mississippi or its tributaries sometimes were centered on a small mound or two, platforms or burial mounds. Of
these, the best-known and biggest was a place along the Arkansas
River near present-day Little Rock, named Toltec Mounds by
American travelers.

The Toltec site is an impressive place to visit, with two of its
eighteen four-sided earthen stage-mounds, or pyramids, reaching
heights of forty to fifty feet. All of these are crowded into a one-
hundred-acre space bounded on one side by a bayou and surrounded
on the others by a semicircular ditch and earthen embankment, a
boundary demarcating the sacred space within from the profane
world outside. It wasn't a defensive feature, and the pyramids inside, as best archaeologists can tell, were not home to elite leaders
but, rather, elevated stages for special community ceremonies, ritual

performances, and feasts probably hosted but not "owned" by high-ranking leaders. The pyramids were meant to be visually impressive and perhaps to hide the tenuous balancing act that the ritual leaders were performing atop the mound. One of the highest pyramids was also intended to trick the eye: It was a narrow platform built up against the bayou that didn't take as much labor to build as its height might suggest.

Spilling down the faces of some of these theatrical stages are the remains of feasts—animal bones and cooked plants—mixed with crystals and bits of craft materials used in the events. Presumably, some higher-ups and religious specialists resided at this center, but most—probably no more than a few thousand—lived in farmsteads and hamlets scattered across the rural floodplain of the Arkansas River, held together by shared experiences and memories of the monumental center with its powerful political-religious hosts.

Toltec dates from about 700 to sometime in the eleventh century, when, for reasons that remain unknown, Toltec and the entire central Arkansas River region was completely abandoned. Where did the people go? Farther up the river, similar but much more modest ceremonial-mound centers were on the rise, and the Toltecans might have gone there. However, most archaeologists believe, based in part on pottery styles, that the modest upper-river neighbors were Caddoans.

Coincidentally, the year 1000 saw the appearance of some pots, if not potters, in the Toltec mold at and near the burgeoning village of Old Cahokia, three hundred miles to the north, which suggests that some Toltecans went north. If they did, and if even a few moved to Old Cahokia, not only would they have appeared as exotic strangers in a new land, but they might have transplanted their vibrant memories of pyramid-related ceremonies and mound-building practices to their new home. This combination of the cultural power of immigrants and the economic base of Old Cahokia, with its access to large amounts of easy-to-farm river bottom, was a recipe for explosive growth. That explosion might have been sparked early one morning in 1054.

On that morning, recorded by a Chinese astrologer as July 4, a brilliant new luminary appeared in the sky. It was a "guest star," a supernova, a visitor in the constellation Taurus, visible today with a high-powered telescope as the Crab Nebula.[3] One of only fifty supernovas ever recorded—only three in our own Milky Way galaxy—this nuclear detonation was the last gasp of a dying star. The inaudible explosion discharged a billion times more energy than the small star had previously emitted, and that morning a brilliant beacon—four times brighter than Venus—appeared in the daylight adjacent to a crescent moon.

It was a new day in more ways than one. For the next twenty-three days, the guest star was visible both night and day around the world. It remained a prominent feature of the night sky for the next two years. Few would have missed the supernova of 1054. For ancient peoples known to watch the skies carefully, a brand-new star that shone, initially, day and night was likely viewed with some combination of wonderment, confusion, and horror. What might the star portend?

Whatever it might have meant to the native peoples, a New Mexican Mimbres valley potter commemorated the celestial event by painting a pot with a star at the foot of a crescent-shaped rabbit, a representation of the rabbit many indigenous North Americans believed resided in the moon. Ancient rock art in Arizona also appears to illustrate the supernova, as do petroglyphs in Missouri, which show the moon and supernova astride rabbit tracks.[4] And in Chaco Canyon, New Mexico, a map of the night sky in July 1054 was painted on the sandstone cliffs above a palatial-sized, multistory Great House called Peñasco Blanco, under construction at about the same time in the middle of the eleventh century. The pictograph shows the exploding star next to a crescent moon and a human hand, the latter possibly representing a group of stars still known among Plains Indians today as the Hand constellation. Also in Chaco Canyon, construction began around this time on a massive new kiva, an underground ceremonial building, now called Casa Rinconada, just south of the largest Great House, Pueblo Bonito.[5] The kiva, dated by archaeologists by counting the tree rings in its roof timbers, is noted for its many astronomical alignments.

Such a flurry of acts to commemorate this great celestial phenomenon is, oddly, not matched elsewhere around the world. No record of the supernova survives from the Islamic and Christian scholars of Europe, Africa, the Near East, India, or Southeast Asia. Possibly, the records of the various small kingdoms that dotted the Old World at the time have not survived. Then again, it may be no coincidence that Byzantium's patriarch formally split with the Roman Catholic Church in July 1054, as the supernova was shining in the Mediterranean sky—perhaps a sign from God.

On the other side of the world from the Chinese imperial capital of Kaifeng, nine hundred miles east-northeast of Chaco Canyon, and thirteen hundred miles from Toltecan Tula, great change came to Old Cahokia. The small houses and family courtyards of the large town—home to more than a thousand native villagers—were razed. Over a short period, possibly weeks or months, the pole-frame houses were dismantled; their remains were covered over with earth; and the old courtyards were, for all intents and purposes, obliterated. Then the city of New Cahokia was built atop the former village in what may constitute the first government-sponsored urban renewal project on the continent, north of Mexico. Construction crews built new houses, probably prefabricated elsewhere, over the sites of former courtyards. Each of the new houses sported a golden-yellow thatched roof, hipped and brought to a sharp ridge-line peak. Whole new neighborhoods were built in this way, each around a plaza and its center post, which marked the neighborhood commons.

Each neighborhood was probably associated with one or two earthen pyramids that were constructed across the razed landscape. These new pyramids, judging from those excavated, were built of heavy river-bottom clay, mined on-site. The clay was carefully laid in thin layers of alternating light and dark colors, then compacted by human feet and, perhaps, wooden pestles. Specially processed light-colored sand was sometimes added to the flat summits as a ritual purification, then covered with the dark clay. Atop these dark brown or black pyramids large domiciles, halls, temples, and council chambers were built. Scores of such pyramids were under construction after 1054, all arrayed—along with their attached neighborhoods of golden-roofed houses—around a brand-new inner pyramid-plaza complex.

Archaeologists are still in the process of measuring the historical tear in the cultural fabric of native tradition that followed, but a few recent findings are helpful in understanding what might have happened. Besides the planned conversion of Cahokia from a big village to a super-sized city, the sudden changes of the mid-eleventh century involved the physical displacement of thousands—possibly tens of thousands—of people. Most of that was a consequence of people relocating to the new urban spaces of the rebuilt capital city for what they might have perceived as a better life. Some portions of the forest- and prairie-covered interior of Missouri and Illinois were emptied, opening up miniature vacant zones where Wood-land peoples had previously resided. Elsewhere, particularly along the fertile river bottoms, the changes were less extreme.

But at the center, the change was striking. New Cahokia's spa-cious grounds were superimposed on, and in some places physically buried the remains of, the entire site of Old Cahokia. Based on the most conservative estimates, the city covered at least three times the total area of the old town. Four to five times is probably more accurate, but New Cahokia was so large—covering three to five square miles—that archaeologists have yet to probe many portions of it. Its centerpiece was an open fifty-acre Grand Plaza, surrounded by packed-clay pyramids.

The size of thirty-five football fields, the Grand Plaza was at the time the biggest public space ever conceived and executed north of Mexico. Built with earth dug from ridges or from designated "borrows"—areas that would later be refilled or used as reservoirs—the Grand Plaza shows signs of careful engineering to allow for drainage. At its slightly higher north end, New Cahokia's central platform mound was elevated skyward. Initially, it was an impressive twenty-foot-high packed-clay pyramid. Just a hundred and fifty years later, it would reach a height of one hundred feet to become the New World's third-largest pyramid. In terms of mass, it was surpassed only by the Pyramid of the Sun at Teotihuacán and the great pyramid at Cholula, in Mexico. It was at least as large as and possibly larger than the Huaca del Sol in Peru, at the city of Moche, which was mostly destroyed by gold-seeking Spanish looters in the seventeenth century.

The latest radiocarbon dating places the construction of New Cahokia at about 1050. The closeness of that date to the appearance of the supernova in 1054 has prompted some archaeologists and historians to question whether the astronomical event could have caused or somehow contributed to the momentous changes that took place in the Mississippi River valley. Certainly, the result of the construction of New Cahokia was the beginning of what archaeologists today call Mississippian culture, which spread in one form or another across eastern North America from Minnesota's lakes to Louisiana's swamps and from the eastern Plains to the

Atlantic. New towns were founded shortly thereafter, populated by people who grew corn, built rectangular pyramidal mounds and flat plazas, and crafted or decorated objects with images of sky and earth gods and godlike ancestors. Whether the supernova played a role or not, the point remains: Something significant happened in the American Midwest a thousand years ago.

3

WALKING INTO CAHOKIA

IT'S DIFFICULT TO KNOW exactly what Cahokia was like at its height, in part because of how eroded and damaged its pyramids and plazas look today. Modern development has taken a toll. An old four-lane highway slices through the inner precinct at the foot of the large pyramid. Just north, an interstate highway cuts through another former plaza. Not so long ago, almost half of the Grand Plaza was covered by a residential subdivision (at the time, no one knew it was the central plaza). Some sixty trim little houses, built in the 1940s, were sprinkled in the middle of the sacred core of the site, sometimes called "downtown Cahokia." In the 1960s, one of the new residents even built an in-ground swimming pool in his backyard, at the foot of the great pyramid.

The state of Illinois later bought the subdivision in the early 1980s in order to include the area in the Cahokia Mounds State Historic Site, and today the houses are gone and the swimming pool is filled in. But scattered commercial enterprises as well as modern residential sprawl still ring the outer edges of the ancient city. All but the 9 or 10 largest pyramids had been damaged as a result of modern farming practices and erosion by the time the state bought the central portion of the site. Of Cahokia's more than 120 mounds, only about half remain in anything near their former proportions. The 45 mounds of the East St. Louis group just south and west of the main group were all destroyed, as were the 26 pyramids formerly on the western bank of the Mississippi River in St. Louis. The last and biggest of the St. Louis monuments, appropriately called the Big Mound, came down just after the Civil War. Even Cahokia's great central pyramid, Monks Mound—the largest such monument in North America, with a total volume in excess of 25 million cubic feet and covering approximately fifteen acres—is today falling down because of erosion or human interference or both.

Given the destruction, imagining the size of the sprawling complex of ancient Cahokia is difficult but still worth attempting. Depending on how one defines the limits of the site, Cahokia covers somewhere between three and five square miles; this does not include the adjacent complexes at East St. Louis and St. Louis, each of which covers perhaps half a square mile or more (the St. Louis site being the lesser of the two). Subtracting plaza space and sparsely occupied areas leaves almost one square mile of high-density residential area. Extrapolating from known numbers of houses and approximate family size produces a population estimate for early New Cahokia (not including the outer suburbs) of between ten thousand and sixteen thousand people. If this estimate is correct, New Cahokia was about the size of an average ancient Mesopotamian city-state (albeit spread out quite a bit more than Uruk, Babel, Tell Brak, Ur, and so forth), close to that of early Andean capitals (Moche, Tiwanaku, Wari), and bigger than the initial capital built atop Monte Albán. For a more contemporary comparison, New Cahokia was more than double the size of the original capital of Washington, D.C., when the government relocated there in 1800.[1]

The scale of the historic happenings along the Mississippi River was not lost on the first Euroamerican visitor to write about Cahokia, a young lawyer-frontiersman who corresponded with aging former president Thomas Jefferson. In a letter dated 1813 (and later in his memoirs), Henry Marie Brackenridge proclaimed himself astonished and awestruck at the number and size of the earthen pyramids clustered in a several-square-mile area in and opposite the French-American gateway city of St. Louis. At the time of his visit, there were still twenty-six mounds just outside Red City, one Plains Indian group's name for St. Louis after the red-haired William Clark was posted there as an Indian agent following his trip up the Missouri River with Meriwether Lewis.

Brackenridge had heard the accounts of earlier pioneers and had talked with William Clark's brother, Revolutionary War hero George Rogers Clark, who had asked Chief Ducoign of the Algonkian-speaking Illini Indians about some mounds south of Cahokia. They were "the works of their forefathers," George was told, "formerly as numerous as the trees in the woods."[2]

Young Brackenridge had visited the St. Louis Indian mounds many times, including the Big Mound. A landmark thirty-four feet high atop a prominent bluff overlooking the Mississippi River north of town, it had not the usual flat summit but a "ridgetop" shape, like the roof of a house or barn. French colonists called it Le Grange Terre, "the earthen barn." One day in 1811, Brackenridge crossed the river at St. Louis, having heard rumors of more ancient mounds on the Illinois side. Sure enough, within fifteen minutes of landing on the Mississippi's eastern shore, he walked into the middle of more than forty-five earthen monuments "resembling enormous haystacks scattered through a meadow" on a floodplain terrace that would a few years later become the city of East St. Louis.[3]

In the East St. Louis group, there was an "earthen barn" even bigger than the Big Mound: the forty-foot-high Cemetery Mound. Brackenridge stood atop one pyramid and looked toward the eastern horizon—a "level plain," he wrote, covered in prairie grass—to the landlocked eastern river bluffs, "dimly seen at the distance of six to eight miles." The pyramids trailed off to the north-northwest along the banks of Cahokia Creek, and when Brackenridge decided to follow them, they led him past yet another ridgetop mound—the second largest of the lot, in fact, at forty feet high, like its East St. Louis counterpart. From the summit of this tumulus, later named the Powell Mound, he would have seen many more mounds off to the east exposed beneath the burnt stubble of wild prairie grasses.

Brackenridge hiked through the burned prairie a further mile and a half toward what he scarcely would allow himself to believe. The path took him into the midst of the ruins of an ancient city, with large symmetrical pyramids everywhere. He later recounted: "When I reached the foot of the principal mound, I was struck with a degree of astonishment, not unlike that which is experienced in contemplating the Egyptian pyramids. What a stupendous pile of earth!" Brackenridge was standing at the north end of the Grand Plaza, having walked through former residential neighborhoods of the ancient city's west end. Now he was in the heart of the city, and the ordered layout of all that he had seen became apparent to him. "I could trace with ease any unevenness of surface," he wrote, "so as to discover whether it was artificial or accidental. I everywhere observed a great number of small elevations of earth, to the height of a few feet, at regular distances from each other, and which appeared to observe some order."[4]

The perceptive young explorer concluded "that a very populous town had once existed here, similar to those of Mexico." Brackenridge compared what he saw to what was then the largest city in North America: "If the city of Philadelphia and its environs were deserted," he wrote, "there would not be more numerous traces of human existence. The great number of mounds, and the astonishing quantity of human bones, every where dug up, or found on the surface of the ground, with a thousand other appearances, announce that this valley was at one period, filled with habitations and villages."[5]

Brackenridge encountered a small group of French Trappist monks whose cabins and chapel had been built atop a mound just west of the largest pyramid—later named Monks Mound for them—where they had planted gardens and orchards. They had come to the middle of an ancient civilization to avoid the modern one. At that time, the great pyramids of Cahokia remained lost in the vegetation and haze of the Mississippi River bottom just three miles from the booming frontier city of St. Louis. Brackenridge wrote Jefferson, befuddled: "When I examined it in 1811, I was astonished that this stupendous monument of antiquity should have been unnoticed by any traveler: I afterwards published an account in the newspapers of St. Louis, detailing its dimensions, describing its form, position &c." However, his description, which he "considered a discovery, attracted no notice."[6]

One's encounter with New Cahokia at the height of its grandeur nine centuries ago would have been considerably different from Brackenridge's and even more so from the experience today. It is possible, though, to imagine a traveler's journey into the central city from a distance of, say, thirty miles to the east, where Cahokia's extensive farming district began. If the traveler set off on foot at sunrise, it would take the better part of two days to make it into downtown Cahokia.

He begins by walking westward along one of many well-worn foot highways (most of which, as with Rome, led to Cahokia), the morning sun casting long shadows across patches of prairie grass or deciduous forest interspersed with fields of corn, squash, local grains, and sunflowers. The trail widens and cuts between larger fields, woodlots, and an occasional village, surrounded in turn by scattered farmhouses and, here and there, a rural temple complex: a well-constructed and immaculate pole-and-thatch building, a free-standing wooden post, and the adjacent home and outbuildings of a priest or temple attendant clustered together on a cleared hilltop. Around the ordinary home sites, families are well into their morning routines, with cooking fires smoldering in backyards, men and women busy tinkering and grinding and conversing, and children running and shouting outside the small houses not so different from the vertical-log cabins built by French colonists who moved into the region six hundred years later.

In these Indian houses, wall posts are set vertically into the earth. Floors are dug below the ground surface to keep out the sum-

mer heat and the winter cold, so people have to step down to enter through the small doorways. Earth is heaped up against these semi-subterranean houses' exterior walls, and the gabled roofs, covered with thick golden thatch, are brought close to the ground. From a distance, the Cahokia houses would have looked almost identical to traditional *campesino* versions in the Yucatán and Central America at the time (and today). However, the traveler sees that the houses in villages and some farmsteads are arranged around a freestanding, telephone-pole-sized upright post, like those of the temple sites. Sometimes these posts are painted red and festooned with tethered objects, unidentifiable at a distance. He might also notice that the houses display a rigidity of orientation and construction style, as if built in accordance with some rule or organizational principle.

That organizational rigidity is especially apparent as the traveler walks by one of the hilltop towns fifteen miles into his walk. He does not enter the town, but here, visible from half a mile's distance atop a large upland ridge, is a cluster of a hundred thatched-roof buildings in rows surrounding a modest open plaza, which is centered in turn on a large temple that sits on a ten-foot-high earthen platform. Around it are eight or nine small mounds, each with one telephone-pole-sized wooden obelisk projecting thirty feet into the air. Some buildings are homes, with families moving around them, and others are special, larger buildings. From one of these emerges a man with a basket, walking toward the hilltop plaza.

As the trail widens the traveler's pace accelerates. It will take most of the rest of the day to reach the Mississippi River bluffs—the large hills on the eastern edge of the low-lying river bottom—below which the city of Cahokia sprawls. At their southern and northern extremes, the bluffs are limestone and sandstone cliffs two hundred feet high, but east of Cahokia, they are more subtle escarpments of aeolian silt blown there during the Ice Age.

Approaching from the east, these hills are steep, and the small creeks at their base are choked with silt. What forest remains on the steeper slopes is patchy, with large cleared areas, some planted with crops and others lying fallow, invaded by weeds, brambles, cedars, and persimmon trees. Late in the afternoon, groups of people tend crops in scattered fields. One or two hills more, and the traveler reaches the bluff crest. The setting sun's rays reveal a great vista as he stands some hundred feet above the enormous floodplain to the west.

Flat and open below him, the floodplain extends all the way to the distant horizon, where, on this clear day, he can see the bluff edge on the other side of the Mississippi, ten miles away. From this vantage point, the traveler can also see several large lakes that fill abandoned ancient channels of the river. If it is autumn or spring, great V-shaped flocks of waterfowl coming and going from those lakes—some perhaps scared off by hunters or fishermen—fill the skies. Beyond them, the hazy hints of a palatial-sized thatched edifice are visible atop a distant principal pyramid.

It is here, at the bluff escarpment's edge, that the well-ordered space of the district of Cahokia would fully engulf one's senses. Looking left and right along the crest, the traveler realizes that he is standing in the middle of a blufftop mortuary zone. The hills to either side are studded with low earthen burial mounds, thatched-roof temples or charnel houses, marker posts, and mortuary scaffolds that offer the bodies of the dead skyward. A few vultures and a dozen crows mount the scaffolds, flapping their wings and picking at the remains laid there. The traveler then searches for a path by which he can wend his way down and around the scaffolds, mounds, and buildings.

As the sun sets he enters the floodplain. Miles away he can see the dim outlines of grouped houses and pyramids on the western horizon, backlit as the day grows old by the first few of a thousand distant dinner fires. It is late, and the traveler needs to spend the night somewhere, perhaps in one of the small sleeping huts or tool sheds at the base of the bluffs.

Early the next morning, crossing into the flat, wide floodplain dubbed by the French in later colonial times the American Bottom, the traveler passes through several miles of flat and sometimes soggy river-bottom farmland, including great fields cleared of trees and cropped in corn, squash, and sunflowers. These are Cahokia's fields, worked by members of family farms dispersed along the subtle natural ridgetops, one or two every few hundred yards or so. Farms that are home to prominent families have a marker post in the front yard, a well-built thatched-roof house, a circular sweat lodge, and one or two outbuildings.

But everywhere, interspersed among the fields and homes abuzz with morning activity, are smelly backwater lakes, marshes, and flood-scoured mudflats. The traveler wades through the duck-weeds, watercress, and cattails in the shallowest marshes, crosses beaver dams and, every so often, a small wooden bridge, all the while detouring around one particularly large old oxbow lake as wide as the Mississippi itself. If he is lucky, a fisherman will offer to paddle the traveler across in his dugout, filled with his early morning catch: a few fish flopping on a stringer and a turtle or two struggling in vain to escape a tangle of fishnets in order to crawl up the side of the boat's rounded bottom.

The traveler's crossing of the floodplain is taking considerably more time than he might have expected the previous evening, standing atop the bluffs he has left only a couple of miles behind. Bypassing at least one town, another hundred houses around a central pyramid and plaza, he cuts across more cornfields and hops more drainage ditches until he approaches what seems a solid wall of rooftops and shadowy pyramids.

People here, most of them farmers, are numerous. Some move along paths alone or in small groups, others in processions thirty or forty people strong. Carrying wrapped packages, stacked pots, and bulging sacks on their backs, they walk along well-marked dirt avenues skirting suburbs of a sort. Dead ahead looms Cahokia, where black packed-earth pyramids, thatched-roof houses, and open plazas replace fields. The pyramids have sharply angled corners, steeply inclined faces, and flat surfaces topped by one, two, or three imposing buildings: golden-roofed temples, well-built elite houses, small storage huts, or meeting houses mostly rectangular in plan. Other pyramids have two, three, or more terraces topped by multiple pole-and-thatch buildings, with plank steps providing access to each terrace summit, some of which are shielded from view by outer post-wall palisades. Here and there is a circular rotunda or sweat lodge with a thin spiral of smoke emanating from its roof. Sweet scents of cut wood and dried grass are carried by the breeze, replacing the odors of the marsh.

With the sun directly overhead now, the traveler is completely enveloped by pyramids, plazas, posts, dwellings, and people. In the distance, the deep, rhythmic, booming sounds of great skin-covered drums are audible, overlaid by a chorus of singers. Large upright marker posts, some a yard in diameter and many yards high, project skyward from the pyramids and from plazas lined with special rectangular buildings constructed at cardinal angles in perfect alignment to those of downtown Cahokia, still ahead.

Half an hour later, the traveler reaches Cahokia's center, the focus of civic and ceremonial life. Here, between the walls and mounds in the foreground, is a flat public square 1,600-plus feet in length and 900-plus feet in width. A host of people gathered in and around this grand precinct are drumming, moving, and singing. This is sacred space, not to be traversed casually, and foot traffic is directed around the ceremony taking place. Were the traveler allowed to pass, he would see this plaza—constructed of weedless, packed fine sand—edged with the finest of buildings astride the largest of earthen pyramids: the main platform at the Grand Plaza's northern end, the awesome Monks Mound. This black packed-earth pyramid of pyramids—the one that, seven centuries later, Henry Marie Brackenridge would call "a stupendous pile of earth"—rivals the largest in Mexico and Peru.

From the plaza, the traveler cannot see the great pyramid's summit, one of three principal terraces, each higher than the next and crowded with a number of extraordinary pole-and-thatch structures within a walled compound. Some of the buildings are temples. Others are council chambers, sleeping houses, storage huts, and attendant quarters. One is a great thatched meeting hall or a palatial residence. The roof of that building—the largest of all, constructed on the north end of the flat summit of Monks Mound—extends the monument's total height a further 30 feet, for a total of more than 130 feet above the plaza. In front of this building, atop this pinnacle of Cahokia, stand several elaborately costumed people.

One of them moves to the edge of the pyramid. He raises his arms and, in the Grand Plaza below, a great shout erupts from a thousand gathered souls. Then the crowd splits in two, and within minutes both halves run across the plaza, shrieking wildly. Hundreds of spears fly through the air toward what, from this distance, seems like a small rolling speck. A melee ensues, and teams regroup and continue. Throngs of spectators gather along the sidelines and cheer the teams onward in a game called chunkey, which, as the next chapter will show, has much to say about the Cahokian way of life.

4

THE ORIGINAL ROLLING STONES

THE GAME CALLED CHUNKEY appears to have played a significant role in organizing social and political life in Cahokia. But understanding this role can be a complicated task. Archaeological remains say something about the game; that information is enhanced by looking at the way that chunkey passed through history after the Cahokians. When Europeans began to journey forth across the vast expanse of eastern North America, they encountered many tribes that were connected to Cahokia, either by lineage or in some other way. These tribes played the last lingering versions of the once great game, and the stories they told of its history added greatly to the understanding of how significant the game was to their Cahokian forbears.

The return of Meriwether Lewis and William Clark to St. Louis at the conclusion of their historic expedition in 1806 piqued the expansionist mood of the young United States. In the next decades, explorers sent west by the government or privately funded by wealthy individuals sought to experience and lay claim to the vast riches of the new American frontier. They were joined or followed by naturalists and artists, some of whom stopped in St. Louis and sketched the large Indian mounds there before heading on to the Great Plains. As Lewis and Clark had, many of these explorers and others worked their way up the Missouri River, the largest natural highway west. Paddling, poling, or pulling against the river's silt-rich waters, they passed through the lands of the Osage, Pawnee, Omaha, Ponca, Dakota, Arikara, Hidatsa, Mandan, Cheyenne, and (farthest out, in present-day Montana) Crow nations.

Some of these peoples, especially those in the eastern Plains, were populous and powerful subsistence farmers who had lived in large villages for many centuries and supplemented their gardens with bison and other wild animals. But others were more recent immigrants to the Plains whose ancestors pushed westward from the Mississippi valley or northward from the Arkansas valley a few centuries before Lewis and Clark. Some villages were quite large, boasting populations of a thousand or more.[1] Their origins as peoples were tied to Cahokia in many ways, both direct and indirect. Some people may have been descendants of high-status Cahokians who, perhaps owing to political intrigue, left their city for lands beyond Cahokia's reach. Others were probably the grandchildren of low-status Cahokians who had emigrated from their homeland in search of a simpler life. Still others may have been related by marriage or were the offspring of either the allies or the enemies of this once-great center of Native American civilization.

Unfortunately, archaeologists cannot be very certain as to how well the ethnic groups and language families of today translate into the identities and migration waves of the past. Caddoan-speaking groups are often assumed to have been closely linked with Cahokia, owing in part to the presence of so many Cahokian artifacts at the likely Caddoan site of Spiro and in part to possible elaborate ritual connections with the Pawnee, Caddoan speakers thought to have resided in Cahokia's heyday near what is now Kansas City.

Other peoples who appear to have descended from or inter-
acted with Cahokians include the later enemies of the Pawnee: Osage, Kansa, Ponca, and Omaha peoples, who spoke dialects often
termed Dhegiha Siouan. Before they moved into the Plains, these
peoples presumably resided farther east in the Midwest, in regions
within and beyond Illinois and Missouri. How closely any of them
were related to Cahokia is an open question. To the south, in
Arkansas, there were more Dhegiha speakers, called the Quapaw,
whose migration legends tie them to the lower Ohio River region
(if not also to the central Mississippi valley). To the north, the Iowa,
Oto, and Missouri spoke varieties of Siouan languages termed Chiwere; their homelands were probably nearer those of the linguisti-
cally and historically related Ho-Chunk (a.k.a. Winnebago) in
Wisconsin, eastern Iowa, and southern Minnesota.

Also with Cahokian connections were the Mandan, who shel-
tered Lewis and Clark in the harsh winter of 1804, and the Hidatsa
and Crow peoples, who had moved onto the Plains from the east.
Others whose ancestors had been or known Cahokians include
Siouan speakers in the Missouri River region and Caddoan speakers
who originated in lands comprising present-day Arkansas, Louisiana,
northeastern Texas, and eastern Oklahoma. In fact, various ancestral Caddo people built towns just like Cahokians, from whom
some might have descended and with whom others were in regular
contact.

It appears likely that many, possibly most, ancient midwestern,
southern, and Plains Indians were in one way or another entangled
in a history that began at Cahokia. The evidence for this is often
indirect, but it is compelling. And that evidence points toward a
singular moment, linked to Cahokia, that changed human history
on the North American continent. Directly or indirectly, what happened at Cahokia altered the identities, livelihoods, and futures of
Native Americans across the continent's Woodlands and Plains.
Moreover, in so altering these people, it also affected the shape and

direction of European colonization and, later, America's westward expansion. If archaeologists can understand this moment, they will have gone a long way toward explaining the historical causes and consequences of civilization's early stages. And they will have added a new chapter to the story of America.

In order to understand the all-important Cahokian moment, archaeologists look to the material evidence of cultural contacts, conflicts, alliances, and conversions. Such evidence is more readily available than one might think. This brings us back to the game, involving a rolling stone, called chunkey by widely separated indigenous groups and described by the first explorers, artists, and naturalists of the American West. As it turns out, chunkey, as it was played from southern Montana to South Carolina, has its roots in Cahokia's big bang. Indeed, it may have been one of the primary vehicles whereby a new politics and a new religion spread from the Mississippi River heartland. In the eleventh century, Cahokians may have won the hearts and minds of distant people through this game, which was much more than a way of passing time.

Originally, chunkey was probably a version of an even earlier children's game called hoop-and-pole. In one form or another, hoop-and-pole was a nearly universal North American diversion not unlike darts, except that opponents—usually two children—attempted to throw sticks or shoot arrows through the center of a rolling wooden hoop. Chunkey seems to have been a very distinctive variant of hoop-and-pole, possibly with different rules. As witnessed by wayfaring artists George Catlin, Rudolph Kurz, and others, chunkey was also usually a contest between two adults or children. At that time, it was also sometimes played in conjunction with or in between major stickball, or lacrosse, tournaments.

By the time European and Anglo-American explorers were penetrating the Plains, the most popular competitive game was not, in fact, chunkey but stickball. Over the years and owing to social changes, disease, and population loss caused by the European colonization of North America, chunkey seems to have fallen out of favor. As it waned, stickball grew in popularity. It was a more violent team sport, played by up to one thousand people at a time. The game was like hand-to-hand combat, which was why some called it the Little Brother of War. The rules, according to Catlin and anthropologist James Mooney, permitted "everything short of murder."[2] By the mid-nineteenth century, chunkey seemed tame compared to stickball. In 1876, an aged Choctaw man declared chunkey "very tedious" and wondered aloud why "his ancestors should have taken any pleasure in such a dull, uninteresting pastime."[3]

And yet, originally, chunkey was *the* game, the favorite amusement of most people, and the evidence supporting its explosion in popularity points to Cahokia. In 1492, the time of first European contact, chunkey was played across the South and the eastern Plains, from the Caddoan heartland east to Florida, then north to and stopping at North Carolina, and finally looping northwest through southern Indiana, Wisconsin, and Minnesota and back up the Missouri River. The widespread occurrence of and similarity in its play suggests a common origin in the not-too-distant past, perhaps less then a thousand years. By the early 1800s, Lewis and Clark, Catlin, and others had recorded how the game was played among the Osage, Pawnee, Omaha, Hidatsa, and Mandan. These non-natives made no mention of joining in the game, perhaps because of the total-body workout involved or perhaps owing to the skill level needed to master it. Or perhaps they, like the aged Choctaw man, didn't see its appeal. One European observer thought it a "task of stupid drudgery."[4] Imagine the modern game of horseshoes but with both the shoes and the ringer posts in motion, and you will have a reasonable estimation of the degree of difficulty involved in playing chunkey.

The rules of the game varied slightly from place to place, suggesting that local people did change them through time and across space to suit their own circumstances. Archaeologists are not certain of the original rules. However, in the eighteenth and nineteenth centuries, chunkey typically involved players with special throwing sticks or poles, some eight or nine feet long. Besides the sticks, one of the players would throw a disk-shaped stone about the size of a modern hockey puck. Unlike a puck, however, the stone was rolled on its edge across a packed-clay playing field. In many cases, the ritual preparation of the playing ground, or chunk yard, involved sprinkling fine sand over it before the game. Then one of the players hurled the stone into the field as two or more players simultaneously began running after it. A few paces into the yard the players would, at about the same time, chuck their playing sticks like huge darts after the rolling stone. Points were scored depending on how close to the stone the sticks—or, actually, a series of marks or leather bands on each stick—landed.[5]

In the South, the prominence and politics of chunkey were apparent in the formal playing grounds of Native American towns, described by European and Anglo-American explorers and naturalists who had seen the Choctaw, Chickasaw, and Muskogee peoples playing the game. Among these explorers was an Irish nobleman–turned-Scot-turned-American named James Adair, who traveled through the southern colonies in the 1770s.

Adair noted that play took place "near their state house" on "a square piece of ground well cleaned"—which is to say the town plaza. William Bartram also noted the proximity of the chunk yards to the public and political centers of society. Bartram said that some of these yards or plazas were "600 to 900 feet in length." In the middle stood a "high obelisk," or massive wooden post, erected in a low earthen mound. The game revolved around this post, which was "30 to 40 feet in height" and topped with the town's insignia or other markers of community identity. Nearby were other posts, some used to exhibit enemy scalps, skulls, and recently captured and bound enemies condemned to death.[6]

Not only was chunkey an important affair, as attested to by its prominent venue on town grounds, but there were other possible associations, direct or indirect, with warfare and enemy executions. The game also had an economic component: Of those peoples for whom we have descriptions, chunkey was a gambling game par excellence. It seems to have been addictive. Indeed, it was probably a bigger gambling game than stickball.

Adair stated that Choctaw men wagered "their silver ornaments, their nose, finger and ear rings; their breast, arm, and wrist plates, and even all their wearing apparel, except that which barely covers their middle." Catlin noted, "These people become excessively fascinated" with chunkey, "often gambling away everything they possess, and even sometimes, when everything else was gone, [they] have been known to stake their liberty upon the issue of these games, offering themselves as slaves to their opponents in case they get beaten." According to one southeastern tale, players bet their spouses on the roll of the stone. Rudolph Kurz said the same of the Hidatsa, whose men would "even venture their elder wives." And if their freedom or family were not enough, another observer noted that "they bet high; here you may see a savage come and bring all his skins, stake them and lose them; next his pipe, his beads, trinkets and ornaments; at last his blankets and other garments, and even all their arms, and after all it is not uncommon for them to go home, borrow a gun and shoot themselves; an instance of this happened in 1771 at East Yasoo a short time before my arrival."[7]

Chunkey meant a lot to its participants, many of whom would have learned the game as children. Archaeologists have found both child-sized chunkey disks, made from stone or baked clay, and the more finely made, adult-sized, disk-shaped stones. The latter were presumably the prized heirlooms of whole families, clans, or even entire towns, as described by the Anglo explorers: "The hurling stones they use at present," Adair said, were from "time immemorial rubbed smooth on the rocks, and with prodigious labor; they are kept with the strictest religious care, from one generation to another, and are exempted from being buried with the dead. They belong to the town where they are used, and are carefully preserved."

One's personal standing or place in a community might be affected by the outcome of this game of chance and skill. Some archaeologists suspect that the politicians of the biggest southern native towns infused the play with political or religious associations that served their own interests. At a minimum, this might have included a sense of team loyalty and community identity. Players from different towns would have met in a host town, and the cheering and wagering would split along community lines. There would have been challengers and a home team, perhaps mortal enemies who came together to settle a dispute or prove a point. Individuals or entire communities would have developed reputations for winning or losing, their very identities at stake.

Those identities, in turn, were tethered to deeper cultural meanings, memories, aesthetic sensibilities, and religious beliefs. The game's sticks and stones, moreover, reaffirmed the relationship between the sexes even as they reflected the cosmos. Throwing a stick at a rolling disk had the same connotations as had chunkey's precursor, hoop-and-pole, which involved a stick and a hoop: Adults understood it to be a virtual sexual act. Thus chunkey was also linked to certain creation-and-rebirth stories. In many indigenous North American oral narratives and legends, human life begins with masculine forces penetrating feminine ones just as the rays of the morning sun penetrate the darkness of night. The rolling chunkey stone itself was sometimes specifically likened to the sun moving across the daytime sky, reflecting the belief that the cosmos was in constant motion, balanced between two extremes: male and female, day and night, sky and earth, life and death.

As if to accentuate the idea that chunkey was a microcosm of the greater cosmos, crosses were occasionally engraved on chunkey disks, representing the four directions or quarters of the universe.

Eye motifs were also engraved on some, so the stones might have been likened to the great supernatural eye of a creator god, a heavenly "thunderbird" deity, or a disembodied human head. Such eyes were featured in many works of art depicting masculine heroes or gods, and rolling heads were the central characters of some indigenous stories.

So, then, archaeologists know that chunkey was played in four-sided plazas centered on obelisklike wooden posts near four-sided "state houses" that, in turn, sat atop four-sided pyramids in towns. They further strongly suspect that, from the beginning, the game merged the sensuality of physical sport and human experience in general with fundamental cosmological principles, oral narratives, and community identities via play in public space. Thus, one can appreciate why the stakes were so high. Of course, the original experience, meaning, or stories that surrounded chunkey might have been different from those recorded in historical times, but archaeological evidence leaves little doubt about the profound effects of the invention and spread of the game, whatever its deeper meanings or rules in the past.

While the more generic hoop-and-pole is a truly ancient pastime, probably reaching back thousands of years, chunkey is certainly part and parcel of the story of Cahokia. In fact, the earliest known chunkey rollers, dating to about 600, were found in a restricted portion of western Illinois and adjacent parts of eastern Missouri, including the Mississippi River floodplain wherein sits Cahokia. Beginning in the seventh century, little circular limestone and baked-clay disks—only two to three fingers wide, with opposing flat or concave sides—seem to indicate some distinctly new spin on the age-old hoop-and-pole game. Sometimes in this early period, the chunkey stones are found among the debris associated with important buildings and village courtyards, signifying their communal importance.

At about the same time, the bow was becoming the weapon of

choice, and people in parts of the Midwest were becoming fully sedentary. There may be a connection between these technology- and mobility-related shifts and the sport of chunkey. That is, a new set of tensions and conflicts over access to croplands and other re- sources probably resulted from sedentism. If these troubles turned violent, bows were a better weapon with which to defend oneself, as they gave warriors the advantage of stealth. Then again violence might have been averted by playing chunkey instead. In any event, this connection still predates the rise of corn agriculture and of large, populous towns, which occurred centuries before the politi- cal, economic, and cultural expansion of Cahokia that ushered in the spread of Mississippian culture. So like hoop-and-pole, chun- key came first and New Cahokia second.

Gregory Perino, a self-trained archaeologist, was among the first to understand the significance of this chronology and of the dif- ferent styles of chunkey stones found throughout the Midwest. The later Mississippian-era Cahokia-region stones, Perino realized, looked different from the earlier disks and from other Mississip- pian stones that turned up at southern town sites. He noted that the "Cahokia-style" chunkey stones were delicately crafted and thinned rollers. They were up to a couple fingers (about an inch) thick and four or five fingers (two or three inches) in diameter, and their op- posing sides were strongly concave to the point of being virtually all cup, with little actual mass. Sometimes the stones were thinned so much that they were perforated through the middle, resulting in a delicate doughnut shape.[8] Often weighing less than an ear of corn, such a stone could have been rolled quite a long way, making it dif- ficult for the stick throwers to hit their marks and score points.

The Cahokia-style stones are readily distinguished from earlier, thicker chunkey stones and from later, southern-style stones, which were more massive and had shallower concave sides. In addition to their finely crafted and distinctive shape, many Cahokia-style stones were made from white or honey-colored, sometimes red-banded, siliceous sandstone or quartzite—essentially, the same light-colored sandy substance that many native townsfolk in the South in historic times were said to have sprinkled on their plazas before playing chunkey.

Such parallels begin to take on more meaning with respect to Cahokia's big bang in light of another intriguing pattern, which emerges when Perino's stylistic observations are cross-referenced with the archaeological finds of chunkey stones around eastern North America. The finely made chunkey stones are found first at Cahokia in 1050 and replaced the older, thicker, community-owned varieties in the region; some evidence hints that not everybody had access to them afterward. Perhaps the best evidence for central control over the stones is seen in a pile of fifteen chunkey stones associated with an elaborate burial in Mound 72, dated at sometime between 1050 and 1100.

But the pan-American pattern is revealing: There are no finely made chunkey stones outside greater Cahokia before 1050. Not in Montana, not in Wisconsin, not in Georgia, not in Alabama, and not in either Oklahoma or Louisiana, all places where the game was played at later dates, and where the artists and explorers of the colonial and early American periods saw it played in earnest by people wagering all they owned on this favorite pastime.

The Cahokia-style stones do show up at certain large sites outside Illinois and Missouri, particularly in the trans–Mississippi River area—but only after 1050. Outside the old pre-Mississippian villages in western Illinois and eastern Missouri, people were not playing chunkey—at least not with stone gaming pieces—before that time. At the first southern towns where chunkey stones appear after 1050, the Cahokia-style disks do not necessarily predominate, but they have been found, together with chunkey stones made in other local styles. For instance, at the Shiloh site in Tennessee— more famous as a Civil War battlefield—both southern and Cahokian varieties of quartzite chunkey stones have been unearthed.

The same is true of other southern towns, including Angel in Indiana, Moundville in Alabama, Towasahgy in Missouri, and Obion in Tennessee. The Cahokia-style disks found at these places look to have been made from stones available around the greater Cahokia region. Beyond these places, chunkey stones—Cahokia-style or otherwise—are scarce.

In fact, no local varieties of chunkey stones have been found in the northern states of Wisconsin, Iowa, or Minnesota, only Cahokia-style stones from sites that date after 1050 and, for the most part, before 1200. A few may have been secreted away, kept from "time immemorial," as Adair noted. One such stone was found in far-off South Carolina. Another heavily modified siliceous-sandstone specimen was buried with the honored dead at the Spiro site in Oklahoma around 1400.

All this suggests to archaeologists a clear connection between the spread of chunkey, as documented with stone rollers in the historical era, and Cahokia. There is also a linguistic reason to think that this historical connection might be real: The Siouan-speaking Mandan called the game *tchungkee,* named after the game's sticks (not its rolling stone). The Choctaw people of Alabama and Mississippi also originally knew the game as chunkey, although by the nineteenth century that word had been phonetically transformed into *achahpih.* The same is true for the Muskogean-speaking peoples of Georgia, who called the game *chungkee,* while their counterparts in South Carolina called it *chenco.* Out west, the Pawnee called the game—without stone rollers—*zhahae* and the Dakota *ha-ka,* or *pain yanka ichute.* But saying these words aloud—*chunkey, chenco, zhahae, ha-ka*—reveals their phonetic similarities and suggests a common origin. The branches of the phonetic tree have a common trunk; and although archaeologists are not in total agreement, at least some evidence points to Cahokia as that trunk.

One important piece of evidence in support of this idea comes from a recent discovery by Thomas Emerson, veteran archaeologist and leader of the University of Illinois's Transportation Archaeological Research Program. Emerson's work focused on a series of famous smoking pipes carved in the shape of anthropomorphic gods, heroic superhuman characters, warriors, shamans, and, in one case, a chunkey player.

Found at an eastern Caddoan site near Ocmulgee, Oklahoma, around 1900, the sculpted Chunkey Player pipe is nearly nine inches tall and was made from a block of soft red stone probably around the year 1100. The carved figure is a piece of sculpture that doubles as a pipe. The bowl is drilled out of the figure's upper back, and a stem hole connects to it inside the body and exits out the figure's lower back. The pipe stem itself, long since deteriorated, would have allowed the user to inhale the smoke of the burning tobacco into the lungs.

The artist who carved this piece realistically depicted a man on his knees in the act of playing chunkey. The character is unambiguously male. The hair on his head is tied up in a bun, and he wears circular ear spools. His neck is adorned with a modest shell-bead choker. In his left hand he holds two short chunkey sticks. In his right hand is a chunkey stone, pulled back as if about to be launched forward along the ground. Most tellingly, the roller in his hand is a Cahokia-style disk.

Up until 2002, Perino and others who worked with Spiroan artifacts and artwork thought that this object, like many similar ones, was made in Oklahoma or Arkansas from a raw material called bauxite, which was mined in Arkansas.[9] That conclusion suggested that someone other than a Cahokian made the pipe that showed a supposed Cahokia-style chunkey stone.

Initially, Emerson saw stylistic similarities between the Chunkey Player and two dozen known red-stone objects. Many are smoking pipes carved in what he identified as a "Cahokia style." As a group, they shared a restricted set of artistic conventions or thematic representations. The carving style is exquisite and naturalistic, with proportions and details of clothing, hairdos, facial features, and bodily poses showing a degree of uniformity that identifies them as the work of a limited number of artisans. Yet this Cahokia style of sculpture is found at archaeological sites all over the Mississippi valley, easily identifiable by its distinctively lifelike depictions of masculine and feminine individuals, shamans, and superhuman characters. This widespread dispersion was not easily explained.

Emerson took the next step. He worked with a geologist and an archaeometric specialist to develop, with the aid of the National Science Foundation, a new short-wave, infrared-light-beam method of measuring the mineral composition of rock. Their device is called a Portable Infrared Mineral Analyzer (PIMA for short) and has the advantage of being able to precisely measure a specimen's mineralogy without damaging it. Functioning like a ray gun, the PIMA is powerful enough to determine where the Chunkey Player pipe and the two dozen other Cahokia-style objects were made. Between 2000 and 2003, Emerson and his team published their results: The red stone sculptures were made not from bauxite but from a raw material called flintclay, which could have been obtained only at a single source of stone originating from an outcrop as close as twenty miles west of Cahokia.[10]

Emerson's work made it clear that the carved representation of a chunkey player holding a Cahokia-style chunkey stone was indeed made at Cahokia. So were the rest of the elaborate sculpture pipes. And, in accordance with the pan-continental archaeological, historical, and linguistic patterns of distribution, chunkey itself—or at least a specific version of it—seems to have arisen near Old Cahokia before 1050. After 1050, judging from their possession of Cahokia-style chunkey stones, many peoples across eastern North America adopted the new game. Possibly, it was even aggressively promoted by Cahokians as an official sport, perhaps with a decidedly Cahokian spin to the rules of an age-old children's game. Some archaeologists believe that the games observed, described, and sketched by Adair, Catlin, and the rest originated at Cahokia. Minimally, this would establish chunkey as an example of Cahokia's widespread, pervasive influence on the indigenous people of eastern North America. More than this, chunkey might also have been a mechanism whereby the Cahokian culture was spread.

5

GHOSTS OF ARCHAEOLOGISTS

ARCHAEOLOGISTS LIVE for the smell and feel of dirt. Under the feet or under the nails, it motivates as no scientific theory can. And many of the most motivated—fittingly, the dirtiest of the dirt archaeologists—work in a place known for the richness of its mud: the American Corn Belt of the midwestern and midsouthern states. Here, some of the most hardworking, hard-living characters ever to sharpen a trowel were long ago working at Cahokia, digging away at the central puzzle in American archaeology.

If anyone should be conceded to be the "father" of modern Cahokian archaeology, it is Preston Holder. Holder and his wife, Joyce Wike, a cultural anthropologist who dabbled in archaeology, came to the Cahokia area in 1952, when he was hired as the first eastern Woodlands specialist in the Department of Art and Archaeology at Washington University in St. Louis. There, he was surrounded mostly by archaeologists who worked in the classical civilizations of the ancient Mediterranean world. He and Joyce had been eager to leave the University of Buffalo, where they had begun their careers after earning their Ph.D.s from the world-renowned Anthropology Department at Columbia University, helmed at that time by the "father of American anthropology," Franz Boas.

They found St. Louis a welcome change from Buffalo, and a good place to raise a family, which they'd already begun. In the 1950s, the former Red City—a.k.a. the Gateway to the West, or Mound City—was neither southern, northern, eastern, nor western. It was a crossroads city, booming in the expansive cold war economy but suffering a serious identity crisis. Racial boundaries were drawn in no uncertain terms. Some neighborhoods and even whole municipalities were all black, and others were all white.

Holder and Wike saw beyond such divides. That made them an odd couple in their new home, bohemian to the bone and with a decidedly far-left-wing bent. Holder's doctoral dissertation was an attempt to apply Marxist anthropological theories to the recent history of the Plains Indians. Wike's was a study of the historical fur trade and Northwest Coast Indians. They saw academia as a means to an end, the inversion of the capitalist system they saw all around them in 1950s America. So unconventional were their politics that Wike believed they were red-baited and blacklisted during the McCarthy era, leading to Holder's dismissal from Washington University in 1957.

Holder was considered brilliant in some ways, infuriating in others, and consistently opinionated and brusque. Though he was dismissed by his contemporaries in later years for his politics and his underwhelming scholarly productivity, his students loved him, admired him, and hated him all at once. He possessed charisma and instinctual confidence and was the picture of worldly manliness. Above all, he was a dirt archaeologist's archaeologist.

Holder began his career with a vengeance. He signed on to Franklin D. Roosevelt's massive New Deal archaeology programs in the 1930s, working with fellow up-and-comers like Gordon

Willey, George Quimby, and Jim Ford. Across the South, the Great
Depression proved a springboard to the careers of these academi-
cally trained field archaeologists. They ran make-work projects,
digging some of the best-known southern sites with large crews of
out-of-work Americans.

A boon to American archaeology, Roosevelt's teams of Works
Progress Administration diggers tackled the big Mississippian sites
in the American South: Spiro in Oklahoma, Macon Plateau and
Irene in Georgia, Hiwassee Island in Tennessee, and more. Cahokia
was a little too far north and a little too cold and snowy in the win-
ters to keep the large crews busy from December to March. One
small crew did work there in 1941; under the pioneering female
crew leader Harriet Smith, they dug into the remnant of a small
pyramid on the main plaza, a mound later destroyed by the 1940s
subdivision that covered much of the Grand Plaza.

Smith's dig didn't last long—it was over a few days after December 7, 1941. The team had planned to dig through the early
winter, but after the Japanese attacked Pearl Harbor, Smith's all-
male crew quit in order to go fight fascism for home and country.

Holder also joined the armed forces. He signed up with the
navy and was sent to fight the Japanese. Years later, he would tell
stories about his time as a coast watcher on a small island in the
Pacific. The Japanese had established an airbase on one side of the
island, he was stationed on the opposite side, and the people of
Espiritú Santo, who had practiced head-hunting before the war, were
trapped in between. Holder, intrepid archeologist that he was, apparently convinced the natives to revive their traditional practice, and
they began taking heads again, this time preying on the unsuspecting
Japanese troops. Holder's unusual ploy demoralized the Japanese, and
when American forces finally retook the island in 1945, the Japanese
were all too ready to surrender.

By comparison, digging at Cahokia may have seemed to him

like moving into calmer waters. But the St. Louis region proved an
archaeological challenge owing to the many "rescue" digs that con-
sumed his waking hours.

Holder was not the first archaeologist to dig at Cahokia, nor
was he the first to rescue an important ancient monument scheduled
for demolition. In 1921, an archaeologist named Warren King
Moorehead was the first to take on the problem of Cahokia. At that
time, prevailing attitudes about Native Americans fostered skepti-
cism about the possibility that they had built these mounds, but
Moorehead wanted to dispel the lingering myth that Cahokia's pyramids were natural, as prominent geologists argued. In order to do
so, he hired teams of men to trench into many of the largest mounds
at Cahokia and its outliers, including a ridgetop mound known before Moorehead's dig for its nests of rattlesnakes. Moorehead
trenched right through the middle of this "Rattlesnake" mound until he hit piles of human bones. It was a prescient find, but not until
Holder was its significance realized. Unfortunately for later archaeologists, Moorehead lacked formal training, and his large-scale digging often did more harm than good. But the evidence he compiled
from his digs did succeed in convincing Illinois politicians to buy
a chunk of the site for a new state park in 1925.

While Moorehead and the earlier antiquarians of the 1860s and
1870s could do little more than wonder at the hundreds of human
bones chopped out of the ridgetop mounds, Holder and Harriet
Smith represented a new breed of dirt archaeologists, men and
women with the motivation and know-how to extrapolate information from their digs. After Moorehead, and up to Holder's time,
most Cahokia archaeology had been undertaken sporadically or was
being done by the local self-trained archaeologist Gregory Perino.
Perino grew up in the virtual shadow of Monks Mound, attending
high school nearby in the 1940s. After classes he would jump onto an
open boxcar of a freight train and jump off at Cahokia or some
other archaeological site, where he would surreptitiously dig for arti-

facts. A hero to many avocational archaeologists, Perino was the diametric opposite of Holder. He was conservative politically, morally, and archaeologically, and he often found Holder's methods unnecessarily tedious.

Yet Holder was the best and most passionate archaeologist to be sucked into ancient Cahokia's vortex before or since. What Perino perceived as tedium others recognized as attention to the fine-grained details of context and association. And, of the two, it was Holder who founded, albeit unintentionally, a new tradition of intensive and dirt-savvy archaeology. Beginning with him, archaeologists in the Cahokia region began to look for the evidence that would enable them to deduce how people in all levels of society lived out their lives. No more would digging mounds alone be thought sufficient to understanding Cahokia. Holder was the first person working there to recognize the invaluable if mundane treasures hidden in the house outlines and garbage deposits of ordinary people. But it would be left to others to fully develop his work, as Holder was fired by Washington University just as his Cahokia research was beginning to produce landmark results.

After his 1957 dismissal, Preston Holder and Joyce Wike left the study of Cahokia behind. Before they left, they met with Holder's heir apparent, an ambitious young academic from the University of Chicago named Melvin Fowler. It was Fowler's new job at the Illinois State Museum to orchestrate archaeological efforts in Illinois, particularly around Cahokia. Fowler remembered the couple's visit, in part because of what they told him about one of Holder's most important discoveries: a mass burial in a small ridgetop mound, not unlike the one accidentally found by Moorehead years earlier. It was a prophetic meeting between Holder, the father of modern Cahokia archaeology and Fowler, who would later be known as the dean of Cahokia archaeology. Just a few short years later, he would make his own discoveries in a little ridgetop tumulus at Cahokia called Mound 72.

But before he could understand just how important Holder and Wike's ridgetop discovery was, Fowler would need to organize a group of dirt archaeologists to contend with the biggest threat yet to Cahokia archaeology. As it turned out, the same McCarthy-era hot-button political issues that had led to Preston Holder's dismissal had also led President Eisenhower to call for a new interstate highway system to coordinate American strategy should the cold war turn hot. Highways, thought Eisenhower, were key to defending America against the ultimate nuclear confrontation with the Soviets. Interstate highways, like the autobahns he had traveled while invading Nazi Germany, were needed, he thought. With these, men and matériel could be moved quickly, and on certain stretches airplanes could land to resupply American defenders.

So it came to pass that St. Louis would once again be a gateway city, as it had been in the early 1800s, this time for Eisenhower's highway system. Not one but five interstate highways were planned to pass through some portion of the Mound City and the opposing Mississippi River bottoms, where Brackenridge had walked alone 150 years before into the heart of Cahokia. By 1960, an army of road graders were driving into the ancient city from the east, clearing land and leveling the terrain for Eisenhower's new highways.

A small part of central Cahokia was state-owned, thanks to Warren Moorehead's efforts in the 1920s. The rest of it, along with any outlying town, cemetery, or village that fell within the highway right-of-ways, was threatened with destruction. In the late 1950s and early 1960s, there were no laws to protect even the most significant of archaeological sites, mounds, or sacred spots. But since the Cahokia site's central precinct was already an Illinois state park, highway department engineers laid out the new interstate alignment just north of Monks Mound, placing much of the highway in a low-lying ancient lake bed with an east–west orientation through which passed Cahokia Creek. In addition, the engineers planned to build exit and entrance ramps and new overpasses for previously existing roads. Ramps and road realignments would pass through the downtown portion of the ancient complex. A host of other outlying sites, many connected to Cahokia, were also slated for destruction.

Fowler and other archaeologists needed to salvage what they could before the bulldozers and road graders destroyed these parts of Cahokia and various other sites. Fowler took the lead in seeking money to pay for the digs. "[The] salvage financing program of the federal government provided up to one-tenth of one percent of the budget of federally constructed projects for the recovery of archaeological and paleontological data,"[1] he wrote, but that wasn't much money—in fact, it was only enough to get the digs under way. To supplement the meager highway funds and to pay the salaries of large crews from the University of Illinois, the Illinois State Museum, and Southern Illinois University, Fowler sought and obtained National Science Foundation (NSF) funds.

The old days of one man with a shovel and some volunteers digging a mound were at an end. Many archaeologists descended on the Mississippi River floodplain near St. Louis in the massive rescue effort, overseen by Fowler, and began work at Cahokia and a series of Cahokian suburbs and outlying sites. One was the Mitchell site, just seven miles to the north, a dozen neat little pyramids around an open plaza on the banks of Long Lake. James Porter, a gruff archaeologist then at Southern Illinois University, led the dig at this place, whose existence was first recorded 156 years earlier, in January 1804, by the intrepid explorer William Clark. It was a memorable trip for Clark, who had fallen through the ice on Long Lake and almost died before beginning his trip up the Missouri River with Meriwether Lewis. He thought the Mitchell site was an Indian "fortress," its mounds "forming a circle" a few miles from the winter camp of Lewis and Clark's Corps of Discovery.[2]

Much had changed by 1960. The lake had been partially drained, and a new slab of interstate concrete was headed straight through the middle of this pre-Columbian town. So Porter, with the help of a cadre of desperate diggers, attempted to stare down the oncoming bulldozers. He and his team cut and trenched their way through the heart of the site, but they couldn't save it all. Porter watched one whole section be scraped away by mechanized road graders and earthmovers. He was able to salvage a few pieces only by working into the nights on the main portion of the site, using his car's headlights to illuminate the dig.

With that many archaeologists working in one area under such desperate conditions, tensions soon manifested themselves. Some of the crew leaders, such as Porter's good friend Charles Bareis, of the University of Illinois, resented Fowler. Bareis, a paranoid former classmate of Fowler's at the University of Chicago, felt as if he'd been tricked. He had wanted to lead the various NSF-funded projects. Bareis saw Fowler as an administrator who'd show up, look at a dig, and then drive back to the Illinois State Museum in Springfield. So Bareis made it his life's work to redeem himself by outdigging the dean of Cahokia archaeology. Over the ensuing years, he would fill up the shelving units in a basement storeroom at the University of Illinois with great finds that would fall to others to study.

Bareis assumed the job of digging under the former location of Mound 51, one of the series of pyramids removed or damaged as the downtown Cahokia subdivision was being finished in the late 1960s. He and his University of Illinois team were also given the task of digging a western portion of the Cahokia site where an interchange was planned through the former location of the large Powell Mound, which had been destroyed by steam shovel three decades earlier. In 1930, hapless academics had watched in horror as it was carted away. Archaeologists would thereafter know the now moundless site as the Powell Tract, a sad chapter in the story of Cahokia's archaeological destruction.

Other tracts that needed to be excavated in the early 1960s sat just west of Monks Mound and were designated Tracts 15A and 15B, following the highway engineers' numerical system. Here, off-ramps and an overpass were planned to tie into the main four-lane highway under construction in the ancient lake bed (and former Mississippi River channel). That highway, in turn, would slice through the middle of one of Cahokia's principal plazas and chop through the northern quarter of a pyramid that projected into the highway right-of-way. Excavations at 15A and 15B were the job of the Illinois State Museum; to get the job done, its director hired a young Ph.D. from Wisconsin named Warren Wittry.

At thirty-three years old, the tall, lanky Wittry was in his prime. A soft-spoken, delicate man, he was a consummate field archaeologist who had devoted his life to digging. He had worked in Wisconsin, North and South Dakota, and Illinois using techniques similar to those of the New Deal archaeology employed by Holder and his contemporaries in the Deep South. As Holder had before him at Cahokia, Wittry began by stripping the excavation tracts of their disturbed upper "plow zones," the rich surface deposits churned up by the Euroamerican farmers with their horse-drawn and later tractor-pulled plows. This enabled Wittry and his crew to identify, map, and then excavate features—the refuse-filled former storage pits and the floors or depressions where houses had once stood.

Wittry had been hired to excavate two large portions of the Cahokia site—whole residential neighborhoods, an area of about five acres—in two short field seasons in 1960 and 1961. The Illinois State Museum funds were sufficient to pay three field supervisors and a largely inexperienced field crew, the first year hired from the local union labor pool and the second from college students around the Midwest. Few of the crew had any idea of the magnitude of the task ahead of them. In fact, the prevailing view was that the entire complex of New Cahokia, with its 120 pyramids, had been—to quote Fowler paraphrasing Professor James B. Griffin of the University of Michigan, the most prominent archaeologist of the time—"a ritual center where a few inhabitants lived for brief periods of time in insubstantial temporary housing."[3] That view turned out to be completely wrong.

Griffin's flawed impression may have grown out of his study of the surface collections of artifact seekers who, through the mid-twentieth century, gravitated to the highest-density debris fields at Cahokia, calling these concentrations of artifacts and debris "campsites" and "villages" within the larger Cahokia site. Later archaeologists would realize that these concentrations were actually the central neighborhoods or, as Melvin Fowler called them, "barrios" of Cahokia's extensive residential district. Griffin's thinking may also have been shaped by the standard excavation strategies in use up to that point, which involved digging into mounds but not bothering to excavate the mundane residential areas in between. And many scholars still labored under the lingering effects of the Mound Builder myth and were not yet ready to accept that American Indians might have built an actual city along the Mississippi River.

For some, Wittry's digs changed that impression. In the spring of 1960, with the help of his nineteen-year-old field assistant, Alan Harn, who had grown up near Dickson Mounds in Illinois, Wittry began his initial excavations at the tracts, intended to allow him to gauge what they would find once the Illinois State Museum crew began to excavate in earnest that summer. When he peeked under the plow zone, Wittry quickly realized that the residential occupation of downtown Cahokia was much more dense than anyone had previously thought. He sent another of his young supervisors, a close friend of Harn's named Patrick Munson, to the local union hall to hire more than two dozen unschooled diggers. Wittry also hired two other supervisors, Wisconsin archaeologists Robert Salzer and William Hurley. Once they arrived, Wittry showed them the test trenches, and the foursome plotted their attack on what would be, up to that point, the largest excavation the Cahokia site had ever seen.

It would not be easy, and it would take its toll on Wittry, who felt burdened by the immensity of the work before him. Munson remembered how Wittry coped with the task of digging 15A and 15B: After work every day "you could set your watch by his drinking."[4] Wittry's supervisors and crew joined him in this nightly ritual, perhaps hoping to paper over the sinking feeling that their mission, to save what they could in advance of the road graders paving the way to Eisenhower's dream, could not possibly end well.

But merely opening up huge swaths of Tracts 15A and 15B led to significant breakthroughs. Wittry and the others found indisputable evidence of a prolonged and intensive human occupation that began a century or more before the construction of New Cahokia—they had found Old Cahokia, the large village that had been methodically dismantled to make way for the new city. The remains of Old Cahokia's earlier semisubterranean houses, dating from between 900 and 1050, were everywhere, surrounded by trash-filled storage pits, ancient versions of root cellars for storing grain. These were cut through or superimposed by the later footings for the even greater New Cahokian constructions, huge public and ceremonial timbered buildings and defensive walls that dated to the years after 1050.

Wittry had found the remains of a populous city first suspected by Brackenridge. On Tract 15B, three hundred yards west of Monks Mound, there was a giant circular rotunda, a public council house or meeting hall measuring some eighty feet in diameter and dating to the late eleventh or early twelfth century. Once the ancient builders had finished using that building, they demolished it and, on the same spot, built an impressive walled compound, complete with circular defensive bastions along its curtain walls and at its corners. Enclosing more than 6,500 square feet, this wall had been built of upright posts and then, according to Munson's recollections, plastered over with clay and painted red.[5] Inside there may have been a special house or religious temple and open storage space. Whatever was inside, the walled compound showed that it was worth defending against attack.

Over at Tract 15A, half a mile to the west, Wittry's team found the simple post-style houses of Old Cahokia beneath the later prefabricated ones of New Cahokia, the best evidence yet of the city's abrupt urban renewal. In addition, Wittry found what he later dubbed "the American Woodhenge," a monumental circle of large upright posts. At first, during his fieldwork in 1961, Wittry wasn't sure what to make of a series of bathtub-shaped pits that, based on research since, date to the twelfth century. These pits, deeper at one end than the other, were arrayed in huge, overlapping arcs across the excavated Tract 15A. Months later, Wittry realized what he'd found: These scattered post pits actually formed perfect circles. With the help of additional excavations in 1963 by his good friend Robert Hall and a serendipitous finding by Porter at the Mitchell site, Wittry had solved the riddle of the bathtub pits by 1964.[6]

Porter had found a broken twelve-foot-long section of an ancient giant cypress log stuck in the mud in the middle of the Mitchell site. Initially, he was not at all sure what the log represented. It was a piece of a huge cypress tree that measured three feet in diameter. The log, as Porter found it, was at an oblique angle to the base of an oddly elongated Indian trench, one of Wittry's bathtub pits. Possibly it was natural, Porter opined in a note typed right after the find.[7] However, given that it had been found at the bottom of this pit, Porter and Wittry soon realized that this giant post had been used to mark the center of the Mitchell plaza. It was resting at the oblique angle because, when the native inhabitants had tried to pull out what must have been a massive marker post, they accidentally snapped it near the base, leaving the buried end to rot underground.

The significance of the find dawned on Wittry. The bathtub pits at 15A had been the foundations for a series of upright marker posts. When he plotted the ones he had found with those found by Hall in 1963, he realized that they had been the perimeter posts in some sort of huge circular monument: something like Stonehenge or other henge monuments in Great Britain. In any case, Wittry concluded that here, at Cahokia, was an American Indian astronomical observatory similar to those of Europe. He spent the next few years figuring out what the American Woodhenge's posts were aligned to. Wittry and Hall concluded that each of the five or more Tract 15A Woodhenge constructions, whose number of posts varied in multiples of twelve, was a calendar device. The largest, with seventy-two posts arranged in a circle that measured 420 feet in diameter, had also been used by Cahokians to track the movements of the sun as it rose and set.

Here, at long last, seemed to be incontrovertible evidence of an ancient American Indian civilization with a sophisticated understanding of geometry, astronomy, and calendrics—not just an urban population but an urbane one as well. Wittry's discoveries presented to the world a new vision of native North America, one that had an American Indian city in its center.

Still, the academy was slow to accept Wittry and Hall's findings. Another generation of archaeologists, some trained by Porter and Bareis, had been taught to seek incontrovertible evidence of any major scientific claim, and were dubious of the implications. Moreover, some of them were hired as the supervisors for the next major highway archaeology project, run by Bareis and Porter in the late 1970s and the 1980s, dubbed the FAI-270 Highway Mitigation Project after the new stretch of interstate highway to be built in the Cahokia region. Understandably, perhaps, the archaeologists of this project and others of the day wanted to be dead certain before accepting what, to them at the time, might have seemed like a bold claim.

Evidence of a dense population in one part of Cahokia, some

would later argue, doesn't mean a dense population for the entire settlement. Digging in the countryside outside the city, the FAI-270 archaeologists encountered mostly small, scattered farmsteads. Perhaps, they reasoned, the densely packed neighborhoods in Tracts 15A and 15B were anomalous and the lower-density rural population was the norm. Likewise, a Woodhenge, for some, was not necessarily that startling a find. It was a big circle of posts that could be laid out by anyone with a single center stake and a long rope. As such, the Woodhenge was not inconsistent with an interpretation that Cahokia was simply a big ceremonial center, a sentiment that in the 1970s and 1980s still fit well with the prevailing romantic view of American Indians as ecologically sensitive beings who would never have built a city.[8]

Yet other startling evidence recovered during the late 1960s better matched the alternative view of Cahokia as a city at the center of a civilization. This evidence, derived from Melvin Fowler's most important discovery at Mound 72, would become critical in shaping a present-day understanding of Cahokia. Fowler's excavations indicated a society that featured social inequality, political theater, and human sacrifice. As it turned out, Preston Holder had already found that same linchpin, but few knew of it, nor did Holder or Wike tell anyone about it after they left Washington University in 1957. However, in their meeting with Fowler in St. Louis, Holder and Wike had described it in some detail.

The Junkyard Mound was the name they gave to the site of their discovery, made quite by accident. Late in 1954, Holder heard a rumor that a small mound near Cahokia was being bulldozed and human bones had been turned up. What was left of the Junkyard Mound when he arrived in January 1955 lay just a few hundred yards southwest of the Powell Tract, near an old twentieth-century junkyard. The landowner was planning to build a "hot sheets" motel there. But the landowner saw a benefit in allowing archaeologists to explore the site and later named his establishment the Indian

Mound Motel. He gave Holder permission and a deadline: Dig all you want for the next three months.

Working without funding, Holder mobilized local volunteers and avocationalists and began wintertime salvage excavations of the Junkyard Mound. Throughout that winter and into the spring of 1955 (the owner had granted Holder an extension), he focused his efforts on what proved to be a massive mortuary deposit. In the end, he would excavate the remains of nearly 180 individuals. Most had died not in a single event but over a period of many years. Their bones had been defleshed—perhaps on blufftop scaffolds— and then saved, probably in special funerary temples, also called charnel houses, for later interment. They were the remains of family members of some important citizens, ancestors and relatives who were given very special treatment after death.

Holder had his suspicions as to why. There was structure to the deposit of bones, more than met the untrained eye. Holder thought that there might be family groups bundled together, wrapped in fabric, and buried with gifts of seashells and cut-shell beads and necklaces. Off to one side, separated from the 170-some other skeletons Holder had excavated, were several burials he recognized as "primaries," those people whose deaths might have occasioned the burial of all the other bones. These primary burials, he thought, had been made when there was still flesh on the bones; that is, these people had died during or just before the burial ritual. To his surprise, not one of the adult primaries was a man. All three were women. And one of them, Joyce Wike later recalled, had died or been killed during childbirth.

Desperate to finish the dig before the time extension was up, Holder had asked his wife, Joyce, to help him finish the Junkyard Mound excavation in early April. Because she was seven months' pregnant with their first child, Theresa, "I was not going to," Wike remembered, "but Preston . . . never had anybody as good as me on fine work . . . because he had trained me."[9] So she found herself working her way down an exquisitely preserved skeleton—one of the three primary burials—in a part of Cahokia near the heavy industries of the American Bottom.

Breathing in sulfuric fumes from the nearby plants, Wike exposed the female skeleton, only to discover that the individual's head had been removed and placed under her left arm; on the abdomen, a dead infant, probably several months old, had been placed. The next female burial, Wike recalled years later, had died as if "injured by a blow to the head." (The couple's research after the dig confirmed that a person who dies an extremely painful death "can have a spasm," leaving the hands and the feet clenched "like claws." Something similar has been observed on the Roman victims who died when superheated volcanic gases swept across ancient Herculaneum in the year 79.)[10] Exposing the central portion of the second body, Wike found the most telling bit of evidence from the whole complex. It was an unborn fetus, head down and still in the woman's abdomen.

When Holder found out that he would have to leave Washington University, he sent his notes to his colleague James Griffin.[11] In them, Holder explained the discovery as a case of human sacrifice followed by a commemorative disposal of all the bones from one or more ancestral temples. This was an honored burial, he believed, as the pregnant woman had been wearing rare copper-covered ear ornaments (known as earspools), and the entire lot was showered in seashells and seashell jewelry.

Holder's excavation records offered another clue to the significance of this discovery. Besides the three women, the fetus, and the infant, he noted, there were several other skeletons of those who had died at the same time—one or two other infants, two adolescents, and a dog—but there were no men. That fact would prove more important than even Holder or Wike realized. In the ancient Mississippian world, as in the Native American communities of the

South encountered by the earliest European explorers, status and rights were reckoned through the female, not the male, bloodline. In such matrilineal societies, only the relatives of the mother counted as one's kin. A leader or ruler who inherited an office would do so, typically, by virtue of his or her mother's blood connection to a prominent family. The mass interment in the Junkyard Mound, it seemed, could have included all the members, past and present, of a single bloodline, including both the ancestors, whose bundled bones were piled on the floor, and the female "primaries," who might have been the mothers to possible family heirs—the adolescents, the infants, and the unborn fetus. Nothing like this had been found before in North America.

However, as in most civilizations around the world, lineages were related by blood or marriage to many other lineages, including the ruling family's bloodline. As a result, there would be many potential heirs to any single political office. Such a situation was good from one point of view, as it meant that there were enough heirs from whom to choose successors to the office of high priest, chief, or ruler. However, this situation also led to political competition and, sometimes, intrigue, espionage, and even assassination. Would-be heirs from one lineage realized that they could better their chances of assuming office if they eliminated the heirs from some other lineage. The result, if carried to an extreme, was a kind of ceremonious murder. One's worst political enemy, if one was a member of a high-status kin group, was one's nearest relative.

Instances of high-status fratricide are known from almost all continents, usually involving single individuals killing their brothers or other individual claimants to office. Cases of entire family groups or bloodlines being eliminated are rare but have been found among the ancient Maya in southern Mexico and Guatemala. There, ceremonious political killings involved one faction's members eliminating another faction's claims to rulership even while honoring their high status. Entire families have been found sacrificed with much pomp and grandeur. They were, after all, probably of esteemed status, if not also the distant blood relatives of the killers themselves.

In the Junkyard Mound, Holder and Wike had turned up evidence that suggested a case of ritualized killing and ceremonious burial similar to that of the Maya. There was no way, upon hearing such a description from the couple in 1957, that Melvin Fowler could have understood it all. But in just ten years, he would make a discovery that put Holder's work into context.

6

DISCOVERY AT MOUND 72

IN 1967, ALBERT MEYER, a five-foot-tall artist with a waxed mustache and a goatee, was moonlighting as a supervising archaeologist for what remains perhaps the single most important dig in American archaeology north of Mexico. Meyer had talked his way into working on the dig, opening up a small earthen mound in the middle of the five-square-mile Cahokia site.[1] It was a fortuitous match of abilities, as Meyer had the skills to produce superb maps and drawings of complicated arrangements of human skeletons. And there turned out to be plenty of skeletons to draw in this little tumulus.

By accident, it seems, the archaeologists working for Melvin Fowler had come upon the remains of an extraordinary series of burials and mass graves in and beneath an odd little mound that dated, they would later realize, to a few years after the big bang of 1050. They understood immediately the importance of their finds. Many bodies buried together suggested to them planned killings, executions, or ceremonial sacrifices and a society characterized by inequality, power struggles, and social complexity. Small-scale societies were not known to engage in such gruesome spectacles. The archaeologists digging this tumulus, known to them only by its number, Mound 72, realized that their finds were comparable in some ways to those from the Royal Cemetery of Ur in Mesopotamia, from Nubian king burials in the Sudan, and from Shang-period tombs of ancient Chinese rulers. So Fowler focused his funding and his crews on Mound 72. Later that year, and over the course of the next four, they expanded their excavations, hiring Al Meyer as a supervisor.

On the heels of Warren Wittry's 1960s discoveries of a new, populous ancient city that featured oversized buildings, defensive compounds, and a Woodhenge, there was a buzz surrounding the potential of Cahokian archaeology. In the late 1960s and early 1970s, a new chronological sequence was constructed based on recently salvaged archaeological data. This was a new story. The speculation was that the populations drawn into New Cahokia were subsequently "Mississippianized" and that their acculturation climaxed in the construction of a Woodhenge, great pyramids, and a defensive wall around the city's core precinct. But no one offered a good explanation of why this had happened. What kind of urbanizing process could explain an American Indian city?

The prospects kept drawing Melvin Fowler's attention back to Cahokia. And since he also worked in Mesoamerica, he conceived of Cahokia as a Mesoamerican archaeologist might. Unlike most other archaeologists, he saw in Cahokia a planned city. There were regularities in the pyramid alignments, he thought, and possibly major axes or avenues around which plazas and neighborhoods were arranged.

Accordingly, Fowler obtained additional National Science Foundation funds to begin exploring the overall plan of the site. His crews made the first detailed topographical map of the city, working to delineate its central wooden wall, or palisade, and attempting to locate Cahokia's pre-Columbian "benchmarks," or survey markers used by the Cahokians to lay out their city. The plan was clearly complex and difficult to pin down, since the wooden marker posts had rotted to dust and many of the earthen pyramids were badly eroded. Fowler thought there had to have been Cahokian surveyors who plotted the city's layout. Indeed, Brackenridge, in 1811, had recognized the "regular distances" between pyramids, "which appeared to observe some order."[2] Harriet Smith, in 1941, had noted the regular orthogonal angles of wall-trench buildings and pyramids. And in digging into a portion of Monks Mound in 1964, Chuck Bareis had observed a complex internal structure that he believed was the work of indigenous engineers.

Driving Fowler around one day in 1965, Bareis pointed to what he said was "a little mound that was quite different."[3] It was Mound 72. Fowler thought it looked unusual, too. This was not an ordinary flat-topped pyramid but a ridgetop mound. Its summit, just six feet higher than the surrounding floodplain, had a straight ridgelike peak, much like the ridgeline of a roof, sloping away from the ridge crest that ran the length of the mound. And unlike the surrounding rectangular pyramids, whose straight sides seemed aligned with the cardinal directions, Mound 72's ridgeline was oriented neither north–south nor east–west. Instead it was offset at an angle of about 120 degrees of azimuth (which is to say, aligned between 30 degrees south of east and 30 degrees north of west). Of course, the exact orientation was hard to know, since the sharpness of the ridgetop shape had, by the 1960s, been considerably reduced by centuries of erosion. Beginning in the 1800s, Euroamerican farmers had plowed over this low mound every year, rounding and grading down its contours. Moreover, when Fowler first saw it, Mound 72 was covered in European lawn grass and was regularly mowed as part of Cahokia Mounds State Park. A paved access road cut along the western mound edge, but even then visitors might drive by and barely notice the low mound. To the untrained eye, it was wholly unimpressive.

But in a discussion with Wittry, Fowler realized the potential astronomical significance of a mound whose ridgelike crest was oriented at 120 degrees of azimuth. "That's exactly the alignment of the summer solstice sunset and winter solstice sunrise in this latitude," Wittry explained.[4] Using a compass and protractor, Fowler began looking for the benchmarks of Cahokia's master plan using a draft of his recently completed topographical map. He noticed that his team of surveyors had inadvertently omitted Mound 72. Coincidentally, he thought, this oddly angled little mound was situated a half mile south of Monks Mound right on a possible north–south centerline.

This was the same kind of mound that had produced hundreds of skeletons when scraped, steam-shoveled, or bulldozed away in East St. Louis, St. Louis, Mitchell, and Cahokia in the nineteenth and twentieth centuries. It was the same kind of mound that Warren Moorehead had trenched in 1923, noting scores of piled bones, and from which Preston Holder and Joyce Wike had removed nearly 180 skeletons in 1955 to make way for the Indian Mound Motel.

In 1967, Fowler hired a veteran of Wittry's Tract 15A dig, Jim Anderson, to supervise a crew who would dig into Mound 72 in search of some evidence of the site's centerline. Specifically, Fowler was looking for a bathtub-shaped post pit like those Wittry and Porter had discovered at 15A and at Mitchell several years earlier. He thought that a tall upright post might mark the centerline and might have served as a benchmark for Cahokia's original surveyors. Sure enough, the diggers found one very near the predicted location early in the 1967 season.

However, in the process, they found something more. In that first year's digging, the Mound 72 archaeologists found the spectacular "beaded burial" at the base of one end of the tumulus: two men—or at least their wrapped corpses—lying on the original (premound) ground surface on top of what Al Meyer believed was the rotted remains of numerous animal pelts. In addition, one of the two corpses lay under a two-inch-thick layer of twenty thousand shell beads, more in one deposit than had ever been found in all other Cahokia digs combined (with the exception of a second Mound 72 find). The other corpse had been laid on top of the beads, which had probably been sewn onto a blanket, cloak, or most likely cape, possibly draped over a wooden framework that was used (like a hospital stretcher or a litter) to carry the second man's body to this spot. The fabric had long since decayed to dust, but the beads remained, indicating that the garment measured about six feet in length and had been made in the shape of a falcon or thunderbird. The bird-cape head, wings, and tail paralleled the dead man's body from head to toe. The body appeared to have been wrapped in a shroud that had been tied shut using cords whose ends were knotted and tied off using another bead. Being wrapped in a shroud probably indicates that the upper individual had died quite some time before his burial on the beaded cape. The shroud wrap might have been necessary to hold the putrefying body together long enough for burial. The same might have been true of the man beneath the cape. His physical proportions and orientation were nearly identical to those of the man above him, so much so that the two can scarcely be distinguished in photographs.

Surrounding these two bodies were others. In fact, over the next four summers, Fowler's crew turned up pit after pit and row after row of human skeletons in other parts of the mound. The lengths and widths of the pits were precisely suited to contain exactly the number of bodies interred within them. The excavation of the largest pit was supervised by Al Meyer, who noticed the telltale signs of a tomb originally lined with logs (which had since disintegrated) as he dug around the pit's margins downward to the bones. At the bottom were the remains of fifty-three sacrificed women, fifty-two of whom were young (most between the ages of fifteen and twenty-five). The fifty-third individual was an "elderly" (thirtyish) female, whom Meyer thought of as "the matron," sparking the notion that she had been the elder wife of some man's harem. Since there were no skeletal indications of how the women had died, it is likely that they were poisoned or strangled or that their throats had been slit. After their deaths, the women were carefully laid to rest in two rows and in two layers. Those who buried them apparently had slightly miscalculated the size of the pit tomb needed to contain fifty-three bodies, since they had to squeeze the last few in by laying them on their sides.

This was one of most complex digs ever undertaken in North America, and the sheer numbers of bodies in pits had not been anticipated. After the fifty-three women and various other people surrounding the beaded-cape burial were discovered, the excavators would uncover some two hundred more skeletons. Several pits contained between nineteen and twenty-four women each, all apparently sacrificial victims. For several such pits, archaeologists were able to determine the victims' final moments in sometimes remarkable detail. The lives of most of those sacrificed, presumably, were extinguished nearby, and their lifeless bodies were then carried into the pit, some on stretchers. But the spectacle of human sacrifice had also happened right there, next to at least one open trench.

In 1970, three years into the work on Mound 72, Fowler gave a young bioarchaeologist named Jerome Rose the grim responsibility of digging the mound's sacrificial pit tombs. Rose was a bright young man who specialized in skeletal excavation and analysis. Once at Mound 72, he insisted on digging drainage ditches around the excavations and covering the work zones with roofed lean-tos to shield the exposed skeletons from the region's notoriously extreme heat and severe summer thunderstorms. It was a simple procedure, but it allowed him to record some incredible details.

Rose uncovered a trench in which there were more bodies in rows and layers. This one seemed to date late in the short sequence of the mound's mortuary events (which probably occurred over a period of a few years late in the eleventh century). Here, in what would be called Feature 229, Rose and his helpers found an upper layer of fifteen corpses laid into the pit on stretchers, with some bodies doubled up. The cedar carrying poles were still preserved intact on either side of the bodies even nine centuries later. Study of the positions of individual bones on the stretchers led him to believe, like Al Meyer before him, that the corpses of men, women, and children had been tightly bound in burial shrouds, each tied up with multiple cords that terminated in knotted tie beads, again presumably to keep the putrefying bodies together. They were not ordinary sacrifices, Rose reasoned, but possibly important people saved for this special occasion.

Whoever they were, these people had belonged to a higher status group than the individuals Rose found next. In fact, what he discovered was among the most gruesome burials in the entire Mound 72 complex. At the base of the layer of wrapped corpses on stretchers, Rose noticed two things: first, a decomposed woven mat and, under that, a thick, loose layer of rotted wood. This pit of fifteen corpses on stretchers had a wooden-plank floor. But it was a false floor, as Rose soon realized. The upper stretcher burials had been laid on a mat-covered plank that had, in turn, been laid over more bodies buried deeper still.

What excavators found under the floor continues to challenge archaeologists' understanding of Cahokia. Beneath the honored burials on stretchers were the bodies of thirty-nine men and women who had, without a doubt, been executed on the spot. In the dispassionate language of a forensic report, Rose described this lower layer of Feature 229, comparing it to the other sacrifice-filled pits excavated in the mound:

> This mass burial is distinguished from the four others not only in the lack of care in burial placement but also in its demographic characteristics. Where the previously described burials were all females, this pit contained 16 males, 2 probable males, 3 females, 3 probable females, and 15 individuals of unknown sex. The average age of 26.2 years is also older than recorded for the other pits. . . .
>
> Evidence of violence also distinguishes these burials from the other mass graves. Three individuals had been decapitated prior to being thrown into the pit. The heads were thrown in before the burials were covered. Another male appears to have been incompletely decapitated. The atlas and skull were separated by 10 cm from the rest of the vertebrae. The fracturing of the mandible . . . and its separation from the skull indicate that considerable force supplied by a heavy implement such as a stone axe or mace was used in decapitation.
>
> The presence of two white chert [chipped-stone] projectile points is also indicative of violence prior to interment. The broken tip of a point . . . lodged [in one body, and a] complete point . . . within the rib cage [of another] . . . could have resulted in immediate death . . . [or] could have been old wounds . . . unrelated to the events leading to burial in this pit.[5]

It seemed likely that the victims had been lined up on the edge of the pit—"lined with fine white sand 2 to 5 cm thick"—and clubbed, one by one, so that their bodies fell sequentially into it. The arms and sometimes the legs of each individual were splayed out in a haphazard way on the pit floor, the bodies piling up—"3 on their side, 3 face down, and 33 on their backs." The toes of many of the bodies "were in contact with the southern wall," indicating that the people had been standing on the southern rim of the open pit, facing their executioners, awaiting the death blows that came in rapid succession. Most shocking of all, the phalanges, or finger bones, of the prone skeletons dug into the fine white sand, indicating that death had not been instantaneous for some.

The archaeologists knew what they had discovered. There, in the middle of North America, more than five centuries before European armies and diseases would arrive to take their own murderous toll, was evidence of large-scale acts of premeditated violence. Today, with newer theories in hand, the graphic violence seen in Fowler's accidental discoveries in Mound 72 has grown even more significant than it seemed at first to Fowler and his crew.

By looking at the two men of the beaded-cape burial, archaeologists have extracted much meaning from the dig at Mound 72. Based on early eighteenth-century accounts of the funerary rites for a dead Natchez leader in Louisiana, the person atop the cape is thought to have been a Cahokian ruler. Rose's analysis, after the skeletons had been removed, indicated that the two men were adults, but not much else is known about them. However, it is suspected that the bodies of people near them were probably honored relatives, sacrificed victims, or retainers killed to accompany the men on their spirit journey into the afterlife. The artifacts found with them may have been offerings to the two men.

The accompanying bodies included at least four adults, probably men, laid adjacent to the beaded-blanket burial. Nearby were seven more adults or young adults, buried with piles of objects. Of the first group, one skeleton was of a person who had died much earlier, his defleshed bones buried as a bundle wrapped in fabric or held inside a basket. A second individual had evidently died on the spot, his body contorted and accompanied by a smashed drinking bottle. Just a few steps away, piles of objects were laid atop the second group of seven corpses. They included a long copper-covered rod (or, alternatively, two or three copper rod or tube segments laid end to end), possibly one or more chunkey sticks, across the waists of the row of bodies. Next to the chunkey stick or rods was a string of very large beads. Just below these was a pile of fifteen Cahokia-style chunkey stones, perhaps originally in one or two sacks. Near that pile was a two-bushel heap of raw, fragmented crystals of mica, a flaky-layered, mirrorlike mineral that could only have come from the Appalachian Mountains of North Carolina. Lastly, there were two piles of more than seven hundred arrows that had been bundled together and buried as quivers. The shafts had long since rotted away, but the tight clusters of superbly chipped stone arrowheads remained. The arrows within each larger group were bundled by arrowhead style or color. The pile of more than three hundred arrows—tipped with mostly white heads—was laid north of the copper rods, over the individuals' heads, and pointed northwest. The other pile, of more than four hundred arrows tipped with darker or multicolored points, was laid south of the rods, over the individuals' legs, and pointed southeast.

Some of the other mortuary deposits seemed to have been timed to coincide with and commemorate the death of the men of the beaded cape and their attendants. This included at least two pits full of female corpses, both packed in two layers with the bodies oriented at an azimuth of about 120 degrees, with the heads and legs pointing right at the main burial complex. One of these, perhaps the first, contained twenty-four young adult women. The second contained fifty-three women. Adjacent to the latter pit were the bodies of four men. Their arms were interlocking, perhaps tied together at the elbows, and all four had had their heads and hands removed.

The beaded-cape burial and the sacrificial offerings were not the first to be made in this spot, a half mile south of Monks Mound. Just thirty yards northwest of the beaded-cape burial there had been a small pole-and-thatch temple or charnel house. Like other buildings and four-sided pyramids of New Cahokia, its long axis was oriented a few degrees off the cardinal directions. Next to it was a telephone-pole-sized marker post. When the post was extracted and the temple dismantled, the bones of people long dead were piled on the now-removed temple floor (along with two pairs of more recently dead people). In addition, the open post pit was enlarged, just ten feet away from the temple floor, and in the larger pit were placed twenty-two bodies in two layers, most likely young women. As if that were not enough, a second pit was found just fifteen feet south of the temple, filled with nineteen more females, including two juveniles, also in two layers. Finally, a low platform mound was built over the top of everything.

While these burials and the platform-mound construction occurred before the beaded-cape burial of the two men, the bodies and objects whose burials coincided with or followed it were all oriented at angles of 120 degrees of azimuth, pointing toward the two men. At the opposite end of the ritual space, near the old temple, a pit was dug down into one of the mass graves of women in order to bury a pile of smashed pots, thirty-six thousand shell beads, and hundreds of loose bone and chipped-stone projectile points just like those buried nearer the two men. This pit was, like the rest thereafter, oriented toward the beaded-cape burial. As Fowler, Wittry, and Bareis had noticed earlier: an odd mound.

These mortuary-feature orientations and associations indicate that those who buried the dead remembered and paid homage to the earlier men associated with the beaded-cape burial. Whoever they were, all burials that followed their interment seemed to reference their presence. Even the platform mound over the top of the dismantled temple appeared to have been partially remodeled, borrowed, or cut away so that it could be extended southward as a new ridgetop tumulus angled in the same direction. Eventually, as the mound was built larger and larger over the years, it subsumed all of the earlier little mounds over the various mass burials and, up until 1967, betrayed an orientation that roughly matched the winter solstice sunrise or the summer solstice sunset. Odd irregularities in the final mound and its earlier stages appear to indicate where people walked to the top of the mound, perhaps to commemorate a solstice, perhaps to remember those buried there, or perhaps to announce to observers who and what this mound represented.

Aspects of the Mound 72 discoveries are also evocative of Mesoamerican customs and practices. Human sacrifice had occurred in North America before Cahokia, at places such as Lake George in Mississippi, around the year 800, where young children and adults might have infrequently been ceremoniously killed.[6] And in the South and on the eastern Plains in historical times, the Pawnee conducted annual Morning Star sacrifices of young women. The Natchez also selected a few women and children to accompany the death of a lord.

However, nowhere north of Mexico was there anything comparable to the scale of executions at Cahokia—4, 7, 19, 22, 24, 39, and 53 people at a time, on repeated occasions. This unique quality of Cahokia's ridgetop-mound mortuary practices grows more intriguing when the number of dead is considered. Some of the numbers seem to make reference to Mexican customs and practices. For instance, the pit full of 53 women, minus the "matron," suggests the fifty-two-year cycle of the ancient Mexican calendar. And there may be parallels between the sacrificial pit with four mutilated men and certain sacrifices to the gods Quetzalcoatl, Tlaloc, or Xipe Totec in Mexico that typically involved the killing of one female and four men.[7]

But what is most compelling and explanatory about Mound 72 is not its similarities to Mesoamerica. Rather, it is the story told by the burials. The mortuary rites here were not done in secret. While Mound 72 sits at the southern end of the central city complex, over half a mile due south of Monks Mound, the location remains highly visible. The hints of ramps to access the top of the various platform stages, and the clubbing to death of people in the open, not behind walls, also suggest staged public performances. This would be in keeping with practices of other Indian people. The sacrificial rites known from the Plains and South were all open, public affairs. These were not considered murders but formal public commemorations.

The burial process began with the readying of the stage. It was important to clean, purify, or line the grave site in order to open the doors between this world and the next. And it is important to mention that sterile earth, pure sand, manufactured dirt, or pelts were all aspects of later stories of godlike culture heroes, including widespread legends of twins or half-brothers. In these stories, one hero brother assumed the characteristics of a thunderbird or a "thunderer" deity and could transform himself into an arrow. The second man sometimes was the alter ego of the first and may have had the unusual habit of spitting beads.

At Mound 72, such a story might have been graphically retold by first carrying in the two dead men, using what appears to be an elaborate stretcher draped with a shell-bead cape or blanket, its twenty thousand beads in a falcon shape, one man the thunderer god-man (possibly even a ruler) and the other his bead-spitter brother. The pile of thirty-six thousand beads and hundreds of arrowheads in the nearby offertory pit, possibly made to honor the two men and the women sacrificed earlier, would have reinforced this aspect of the story. So, too, might have the retainers, at least one of whom was living up until the point of his interment.

But the numbers of people and groups of objects involved were telling: two, four, and seven. Besides the two men themselves, there were also two groups of retainers, two piles or bags full of chunkey stones, and two groups of arrows. And almost every other mass grave in the mound before and after the beaded-cape burial consisted of paired bodies and double rows or layers of bodies. The four individuals laid next to the two men and the nearby headless and handless foursome might have represented the four principal directions or, as in a well-known Ho-Chunk story from Wisconsin, four lightning bolts. Likewise, the seven other corpses nearby—atop which were piled the chunkey stones, bundled arrows, copper rods, and strings of beads—might have embodied the story's other brothers or perhaps enemies whom the hero brothers often encountered in the legendary accounts of indigenous people in eastern North America. They might also have represented the stars of the Pleiades or the seven "brother" stars of the Big Dipper, sometimes thought of as a crooked pole, with the North Star being the leader, literally the polestar. Sometimes these stars were thought by Native Americans to be an access point or path into the spirit world, where the honored dead would go. In such case, the copper-covered pole or chunkey stick might also be a sacred pole, or scepter of authority, laid over the top of the seven night-sky representatives.

Less ambiguous are the other artifacts buried with the retainers of the possible thunderer and bead-spitter characters, starting with the arrows. Among the Ho-Chunk, it was said that after the mythical half-brothers were orphaned, the people took very great care of them, honoring them with offerings, especially arrows. The people "were always preparing arrows to bring to them"—these "children of the sun." This is why, among other descendants and neighbors of Cahokia, arrows were routinely used as offerings of friendship or as a greeting. Beads and spitting were also used as a kind of honored greeting, confusing Europeans, who did not take kindly to being spat on.[8] The arrows and beads buried with the retainers or piled into the offertory pit were tributes to these men from their people. Moreover, they embodied the power of the men and were probably meant to represent the intersection of all the forces of the universe at the grave site.

The arrows give a few more clues to understanding the larger meaning of the central mortuary performance. The northern bundles, tipped with lighter-colored arrowheads, pointed to the summer solstice sunset; the southern bundles, with darker-colored arrowheads, pointed to the winter solstice sunrise. This meant that the arrows balanced the opposing forces of the universe in a number of ways. They simultaneously referred to the passing of a day, the seasons of a year, and the forces of light and dark, day and night, and life and death. As they bundled together the diversity of styles and arrow makers into one collective offering, they also seem to indicate that the beaded-blanket men were unifiers of the diverse peoples and forces of the universe into one society, one place, and one body politic.

The mica crystals might hold another clue to the meaning of the beaded burial. It has been suggested that they could be considered "locatives"—in art and iconography, graphic clues that serve to locate the action depicted in space and time. For instance, various iconographic symbols in southeastern art locate the action in this world, in the sky-world above, or in and under the earth below.[9] Elsewhere, Native American religious specialists used crystals to prognosticate and to see into other dimensions. Hence, if the mica crystals in Mound 72 were locatives, they would suggest that the mortuary performance occurred between this world and another, most likely the land of the dead. By this line of reasoning, the chunkey stones (and perhaps the copper-covered chunkey pole or sticks) might have been another prop in the theater of life and death. Even the corpses and piled bones of the dead might have been props in a staged drama that served the ends of the actors as much as the dead. It was, after all, the living who placed the objects over the bodies and who carried the corpses and bones onto the set. It was they who executed the individuals buried with the two men, lopped off the heads and hands of the four men, and strangled or cut the throats of the women in the mass graves.

Despite whatever symbolism the objects and human remains in the Mound 72 mortuaries may have had, their placement also explains much about the ceremony itself, which was designed as a means of making a statement regarding the consolidation of ancestral and celestial power at Cahokia. The net historical effect of such unprecedented theatrical rites of life and death or past and present may have been to cement ideas regarding religion, sex, and rulership in the legends and lore of many indigenous North Americans for centuries to come.

7

TWIN HEROES

AT THE HEART OF THE DISCOVERIES made in Mound 72 was the pair of burials that likely occasioned much of the ceremony surrounding the other interments. All the evidence suggests that the two men were significant figures in the Cahokian world, though little can be gleaned of their specific life histories. Understanding their story has seemed key to getting a firm grasp on Cahokian society, but doing so has required that archaeologists obtain some sort of map to lead them there.

That map, or at least an important piece of it, was found in 1974 by a young boy in southern Wisconsin. It was painted on the back wall of a grotto, a shallow cave—technically, a rockshelter— hidden at the dead end of a small, rocky stream valley. Amid other glyphs painted onto the walls over many years was an isolated panel that consisted of human and animal figures produced by an artist in a foreign "southern" Mississippian style. These appeared to have been painted on a specially prepared portion of the sandstone wall large enough to hold the entire scene. The artist first sanded the wall smooth, then, to the right, painted a small male figure distinctive in his eyes, chest, and hair ornamentation. Flanking this figure, the artist added a large, dark bird of prey and a turtle; all three looked to the viewer's left. Facing these characters, the artist painted two large, imposing human figures. The effect was a scene in which characters were confronting one another.

For years, archaeologists had been working in Wisconsin in hopes of finding the elusive historical moment when Cahokians encountered their native Wisconsin neighbors to the north. Sites such as Aztalan, near Madison, and Trempealeau, north of La Crosse, exemplified a series of likely outposts, missions, or colonies set up by Cahokians, Cahokian expatriates, or Cahokian sympathizers between the years 1050 and 1200. Cahokians seem to have had an interest in the north, and northerners appear to have reciprocated by emulating or adopting their ways. The Cahokian influence was manifest in the upper Midwest at a time when the northern Late Woodland folks constructed modest effigy mounds in the shapes of birds, bears, and water spirits or panthers. Such mounds appear to have been built in homage to the native Wisconsinites' ancestors, and human remains are sometimes found in association with them. Yet, not long after the Cahokians contacted these upriver people and their Cahokia-made objects moved, effigy-mound-construction practices ceased. Possibly, the locals dropped them in favor of, or in reaction to, a new religion emanating out of the south that was transplanted to the outposts and missions in the north.[1] Other archaeologists believe that there might be local reasons explaining the end of what they call the Effigy Mound Culture.

Clearly, knowing who was doing what and where in the north would help archaeologists determine if and how Cahokia's big bang affected peoples far away from Cahokia proper. In a way, that's what archaeologist Bob Salzer found inside the Gottschall Rockshelter: evidence of the extent to which this singular event had altered the legendary stories and religious beliefs of people far away, in southern Wisconsin. The painted series of characters that Salzer dubbed the Red Horn panel may tell the story of New Cahokia, at least as it was locally understood by this indigenous artist, who painted the panel apparently at about the time of Cahokia's mid-eleventh-century flashpoint. Circumstantial evidence and radiocarbon dates from paint chips and drips on the rockshelter floor all point to an eleventh-century production.

Salzer had a lifelong fascination with the larger historical problems of midwestern archaeology that center on Cahokia. He was raised in Wisconsin and had close friendships and emotional ties to the indigenous people of the state. In 1954 he was adopted into a Potawatomi family; later he was accepted into the Eagle clan and given the name Eagle Sky. In 1960 he was hired to work as a supervisor for Warren Wittry at Cahokia. That experience left a lasting impression, and in the mid-1970s Salzer returned to Cahokia with his own field schools to continue what he, Wittry, and others had started. In 1978, as a professor at Beloit College, in southern Wisconsin, Salzer was sent Polaroid photographs of the recently discovered Gottschall rock art.

The most important rock art at the site, he realized from the photos and his subsequent visits, was the Red Horn panel of pictographs. These were, he later recorded, painted in black on the specially sanded portion of the sandstone wall at about shoulder height. On the left were the representations of the upper bodies of two human or possibly, Salzer thought, superhuman characters, each less than a foot in height, shown with Mohawk-style haircuts, chest ornaments, and elaborate circular headpieces on their foreheads that look like rayed-sun symbols. These two are shown looking directly at two or three other characters to the right that are, in turn, looking back at them. The principal masculine character on the right side of the panel looks to be a slightly smaller human or superhuman male, shown naked above the waist, his hair tied back, save for a long forward-hanging braid. There are vertical zigzag-ging stripes painted on his chest, and each breast seems to have been tattooed in some way to accentuate the nipples. He has face paint or tattoos near his eyes and a couple of extra lines reminiscent of a "forked eye" motif that—based on other iconographic infor-mation from eastern North America—might have been meant to resemble the unique feathered pattern on a peregrine falcon. In fact, painted next to him is a bird, possibly a falcon, that appears to be walking with wings folded. Next to that bird of prey is the other nonhuman character, the large turtle.

When Salzer visited the Gottschall Rockshelter for the first time, he was dubious of the work's authenticity. It seemed too good; and in its detail, color, and stylistic finesse, it was unlike the other rock art. So he sent a photo to his friend and colleague Robert Hall. Hall gave Salzer a quick reply, telling him that he thought "one of the characters was a son of Red Horn or He-who-wears-human-heads-as-earrings." It was an authentic painting.

This interpretation was drawn from and closely matched sto-ries told by the Iowa, a Chiwere Siouan–speaking group west of the Mississippi, and the Ho-Chunk, another Chiwere Siouan group living in Wisconsin, who both believe that their ancestors had used this site since before the time of Christ up into the nineteenth cen-tury. In 1908 a Ho-Chunk elder named Jasper Blowsnake told the legendary account of a superhuman man named Red Horn to Paul Radin, a protégé of Franz Boas, who was then doing research on American Indian folklore.[2] The implications of this possible link between Indian legend and Gottschall's imagery have yet to be fully explored, but as if to confirm the connection, one of the last painted images to be added by someone, perhaps a bilingual person, to the rockshelter was a word or a set of initials placed near the Red Horn panel. Appropriately (or ironically), perhaps, three uppercase letters, painted in red, read "RED."

Digging into the layers of the cave, Salzer found that the pictographs in the rockshelter were just one piece of the larger story recorded there. From the earliest times, it seems, the predecessors or ancestors of the Iowa or Ho-Chunk manufactured colored soil with special properties to use in purification rituals within the cave. Also inside is a small bird-effigy mound of a sort usually built outside on high hills in this part of Wisconsin until around 1050. Likely sacred objects wrapped in hides—probably "medicine bundles" like those kept by later Midwest and Plains peoples—were buried in pits in the earth under the wings of this bird.

Among a miscellany of other such finds was a carved-sandstone head some ten inches tall. Salzer figured that it had been attached to a body made of biodegradable organic material, such as wood or fabric, and had been fitted with a headdress. It had been an effigy man, almost a doll, buried facedown in the colored dirt. Like one of the characters of the Red Horn panel, the stone head was painted with long vertical stripes across the face. More significantly, Salzer's radiocarbon dates of the carbonized wood near the head placed its burial, like the paint chips and drips associated with the painting of the Red Horn rock-art panel, to sometime in the tenth or eleventh centuries.

This dating is confirmed by another cave painting of a lined-face character, known to date to around 1050. In a place fittingly dubbed Picture Cave, just sixty miles west of Cahokia (and a simple canoe trip up the Missouri River), ancient artists painted some four hundred images or scenes on the walls of the deep, dark passages. Many of these images date to the eleventh century, as indicated by radiocarbon dates of paint samples. In one of the numerous images showing warriors in special dress and holding weapons, a male wearing an elaborate arrow headdress and distinctive ear ornaments holds a bow in his left hand and a ghostly human head in his right. He appears to be emerging from a crack in the cave wall, and both his body and face and the face of the disembodied head he holds are painted with vertical black lines.[3]

The ear ornaments of this character at Picture Cave are especially revealing. In the painting, the figure's head is turned to his right, so that only the ornament hanging from his left earlobe is visible. Presumably he wore another on the opposite earlobe. The one that can be seen is a white shield-shaped object with a small slit mouth and circular goggle-shaped eyes, outlined in black with a central black dot for a pupil. A notch is shown in the middle of the forehead, which is delineated by a horizontal line. And then, the most distinctive feature: a long, pointed, and upwardly curving nose. In other contexts, Cahokian archaeologists have referred to such things as "long-nosed-god" maskettes or earpieces, and their symbolism has implications in understanding the official religion of the Cahokians and its Mesoamerican roots. They also seemed to identify the wearer as related to a prominent Cahokian.

Salzer wondered about the identity of the painters of the Red Horn panel inside the Gottschall Rockshelter. The figures look different from the rest found there, and they date to the end of the ritual use of the grotto, a time of major cultural changes in southern Wisconsin, ushered in, it seems, by Cahokians in the area. Perhaps, thought Salzer, the Red Horn legend recorded by Radin may have originally been an indigenous interpretation of actual historical events of the eleventh century.[4] The Red Horn panel might have been painted by a ritual specialist or an elder schooled in or attempting to copy the new Mississippian art style of Cahokia. Perhaps the story of Red Horn, at least as it was being told in the Gottschall storyboard, was changed by the artist, altered to fit the new realities of eleventh-century southern Wisconsin. It is unlikely that the artists who painted either the Gottschall or the Picture Cave art were foreigners, much less Mesoamericans. However, it is plausible that they might have been members of some political-religious movement, perhaps Cahokian priests-in-training or would-be leaders on vision quests, who painted on the walls some version of their cosmology.

If so, then the Gottschall Rockshelter and Picture Cave evidence is similar in at least two respects to the mortuary remains of Mound 72. First, the materials and media of ritual commemorations or social action—whether painted imagery, crystal locatives, or human remains—are also the mechanisms whereby people routinely or theatrically experience and remake their identities, beliefs, and histories. Second, both archaeological contexts point toward the emergence by the mid-eleventh century of a powerful cultural narrative surrounding heroic characters who are identified in one way or another with supernatural thunderbird deities, arrows, special nipple or ear ornaments, disembodied human heads, and the afterlife or underworld.

In Ho-Chunk mythology, there was once a group of brothers, the youngest of whom was called He-who-gets-hit-with-deer-lungs. This odd name stemmed from the fact that he was the subject of some teasing by his brothers, who threw things at him—including the discarded organs of slaughtered deer. But He-who-gets-hit-with-deer-lungs was not an ordinary man. He was a superhuman individual, a demigod created by the Earthmaker. One day he revealed his true identity to his brothers.

"Those in the heavens who created me did not call me by this name, He-who-gets-hit-with-deer-lungs," he told them. "They called me He-who-wears-human-heads-as-earrings." As evidence, he "spat upon his hands and began fingering his ears. And as he did this, little faces suddenly appeared on his ears, laughing, winking, and sticking out their tongues." Likewise, if He-who-wears-human-heads-as-earrings touched a lock of his hair, he could change it into a long, red lock—a red horn, which became yet another name. He also had the miraculous ability to morph into an arrow in flight in order to win races against his brothers.[5]

From that time on, went the Ho-Chunk legend, Red Horn was involved in warring and adventuring with his brothers as well as with his superhuman friends, including a turtle and a falcon.

Like Red Horn, these superhuman characters had special abilities. For instance, the turtle was unusually fast while the falcon, named Storms-as-he-walks, was actually a supernatural sky god, a "thunderbird" who could shoot lightning from his eyes.

Red Horn married a girl who wore a white beaver-skin wrap. Soon after that, a group of threatening giants moved into the area. Red Horn and his mates challenged the giants to a series of high-stakes games, including a stickball match in which the losers would be put to death. Red Horn and his team won, and the giants were slaughtered, except for one attractive woman, called Red-Haired Giantess, whom Red Horn took as his second wife. After Girl-with-the-white-beaver-skin-as-a-wrap gave birth to a son, so too did the giantess. Of Red Horn's two sons—half-brothers—the first was born like the father, with little human heads on his ear-lobes. The second was born with the same little human heads, but on his nipples instead, a description that closely fits the painted masculine figure in the Gottschall Rockshelter.

They were good sons, by and large, although like tricksters of Ho-Chunk lore, they did have a series of misadventures. In those days, went the story, there were more giants in the land, and Red Horn, thunderbird, and turtle found themselves challenged to another high-stakes stickball game. This time, unfortunately, they lost. They were killed, and their heads placed on pikes in the giants' village. But the sons of Red Horn took it upon themselves to seek revenge. They challenged the giants and defeated them, retrieving the heads of their father, the turtle, and the holy bird from the enemy village. Then, through powerful medicine, the brothers resurrected them all. Red Horn lived again, thanks to the sons. Justice prevailed, and order was returned to the land.

The Red Horn saga as told by Ho-Chunk elders has been a source of considerable speculation for archaeologists over the years. How ancient was this tale? Many archaeologists and art historians assumed that it was as old as the people of North America. Radin did not. Rather, he believed that the tale had a more recent history, linked to real events and real people in the Mississippi valley. As with the myths of most other cultures—the stories of King Arthur, Johnny Appleseed, Helen of Troy, Atlantis, and great floods, for example—there seemed to be a kernel of historical fact behind the fantastic tale. Radin, and archaeologists who followed him, believed that the He-who-wears-human-heads-as-earrings and Girl-with-the-white-beaver-skin-as-a-wrap narratives could be traced through archaeological remains. In fact, the most extraordinary of Cahokian mortuary practices involving human sacrifices in the great ridgetop mounds, such as those discovered at Mound 72, were spectacular performances that could easily be read as ancient hero stories involving the bodies—alive and dead—of enemies, ancestors, and Cahokia's royal family.

Understanding the context of the oral accounts makes this connection clearer. As it turns out, many American Indians have some variant of the trickster tales and, sometimes, of a masculine culture hero and male hero "twins" who were of divine or semidivine creation and who mediated between the realms of the supernatural and human worlds. The stories most like the Ho-Chunk's are, perhaps not surprisingly, those of other Siouan-speaking peoples or their nearest neighbors in the eastern Plains, Midwest, and South. For instance, the Iowa, closely related to the Ho-Chunk, told a tale about a semidivine man named Human-head-earrings and his brother, Black Hawk (a pseudonym also used by Wisconsin's early nineteenth-century Sauk war leader). In fact, certain members of the Iowa nation believed that Human-head-earrings had actually lived in the not-too-distant past. An Iowa storyteller in the early twentieth century was reported to have said: "Human-head-earrings was only a man like the rest of us, but he said that when he died his little heads should live always."[6]

And while heroic-brothers and trickster tales are found worldwide, the specific Siouan similarities imply that there were real connections between narrative and history. In versions of similar stories from various Siouan-speaking Indian nations in the upper Midwest and eastern Plains, the culture hero—the Ho-Chunk's Red Horn or the Iowa's Human-head-earrings—is viewed as the incarnation of the Morning Star god, a masculine counterpart to a feminine Evening Star or Earth Mother deity, also associated with creation. Similar deities are known among many North American Indians and are commonly associated with the powerful sky-world deities, thunderbirds, and earthly or underworld deities. In various ways, the duality of male-female or upper-lower worlds provides a metaphor by which people understood creation and the balance between themselves and the forces that surrounded them.

The same duality and balance is portrayed in the related stories of the trickster twins or the half-brother hero sons, typically identified as superhuman or as connected in some way to sky-world thunderbird gods. The twins were seen either as children of the Morning Star and Evening Star or, in human form, as the offspring of a Red Horn–like character and a female hero-goddess, Corn Mother. In one parallel Ho-Chunk story, they are also called the Children of the Sun. Among the Hidatsa, Crow, Caddo, and Natchez, the name of the first boy was, alternatively, Lodge Boy or Civilized Boy. His brother was Wild Boy, Spring Boy, Afterbirth Boy, or Thrown-Away.

Whatever the names, the characteristics of the two were well established. The first was a cultured, mannered, and consistently superhuman son. He could change himself into thunder or rain or, as among the Caddo, cause lightning by sticking out his tongue. The second was, sometimes literally, the afterbirth, the uncivilized, abnormal son, erratic and subhuman, a trickster sometimes associated with the underworld as a spirit or god. In one Ho-Chunk story, the wild boy kills and eats thunderbirds. In Hidatsa accounts, he leaves vicious bite marks with his fangs. Perhaps this is why one Mandan impersonator of the Foolish One, as recorded by the artist

George Catlin, wore face paint showing a frightening toothed mouth (and circular eyes). In Hidatsa accounts, the uncivilized brother also has the ability to spit mollusk-shell beads, while a similar ability is attributed to the twins' father among the Muskogee of the Deep South.

References to the twins in North America are not restricted to the Mississippi valley but are found among the Iroquois in far-off New York and among their linguistic cousins, the Cherokee of North Carolina. Here, the association of the story with maize or corn is pronounced and, intriguingly, suggestive of Mesoamerican inspiration. "According to the usual Iroquois version," wrote analyst John Witthoft in 1948, "maize grew from the body of the woman who gave birth to the Creator and his evil-minded twin." He continued:

> This Corn Mother . . . was impregnated by a man from the heavens, who, according to my Cayuga informants, laid a sharp arrow and a blunt arrow on her body, these forming the good and bad brothers. When the twins were ready to be born, the evil-minded one went in the direction of a beam of light, so killing his mother, but the Creator was born naturally. The maize sprang from her body. Flint, the evil-minded brother, and the Creator grew up together, always engaged in struggle. The Creator made man and many useful animals and plants; Flint made carnivorous animals and enemies to man. Finally, the Creator overcame his brother (in the bowl game, according to some variants), and thus ensured the continuance of man and his world.[7]

The Cherokee twins, also called Thunderers, kill their Corn Mother, as did the twins of the Natchez, as well as those of a host of Mesoamerican peoples. Most famously, the son (or brother) of the

Aztec goddess Coyolxauhqui chopped her up into pieces at one point, a mythical act commemorated in a great stone carving that sat at the base of the Templo Mayor in ancient Tenochtitlán (Mexico City). And, as archaeologist Robert Hall has noted, the Cherokee Corn Mother's name, "Selu," is strikingly similar to the root word "Xilo-" (pronounced "she-lo") in Xilonen, the name of the young virgin Mexican corn goddess.[8]

Hall suggested that such stories hint at ancient links between Cahokia, the Prairie Plains and southern Native Americans, and their distant relatives in Mesoamerica. As inventoried in Hall's writings and propounded by anthropologist Alice Kehoe, the possible Mesoamerican connections are multiple and suggest that influence traveled north to Cahokia. There are numerological parallels (twos, fours, sevens, and twelves), venerations of Venus and the sun, distinctive female sacrifice rituals, an Osage association of north with sky, post-Classic-Mexican-style knife blades made in Illinois, Mesoamericanlike hats, filed teeth, long-nosed-god imagery, and the occasional word whose morphology suggests a nonlocal origin. Even the construction of four-sided plazas and pyramids topped with public buildings might have been influenced by Mexican archetypes, although they also have a long, long history in eastern North America.

The Red Horn saga of the Ho-Chunk and the various other hero-brother stories are also strikingly similar to Mesoamerican stories, such as the Mexican account of the sky lord Quetzalcoatl and his double, Xolotl, who entered the underworld to retrieve the bones of people. This tale perhaps inspired another: the famous creation story of the Quiche Maya, as written down by Maya priests and entitled the *Popul Vuh*. In that story, saved somehow from destruction by Spanish priests, a pair of twin brothers, Hunahpu and Xblanque, were born to an underworld goddess called Blood Woman. Like the Ho-Chunk's Red-Haired Giantess, Blood

Woman was impregnated when the head of the semidivine father, stuck in a tree in the underworld (like Red Horn's head on a pike), spat into her hand. After a series of adventures and ball games against their foes, as in the Ho-Chunk saga, the boys defeat the underworld gods and retrieve and reanimate their father's head.

Some scholars believe that the similarity of these stories springs from a universal human tendency to see the world in dualistic terms: good and bad, light and dark, day and night, men and women, and upper and lower worlds. Others think that the common elements—severed heads, reincarnation, and games in some liminal land—mean that there were historical connections between North American and Mesoamerican peoples. For these scholars, the question is one more of timing and direction: Who influenced whom, and when?

The intriguing details of the Siouan stories, best represented by the Ho-Chunk Red Horn epic, prompt further questions. What about those giants, the thunderbird associations, the red hair, and, especially, the human-head earrings? These are distinctive features of the North American narratives that suggest something more than random retellings of a Mesoamerican myth. Paul Radin thought there was something more to the history of the narratives that suggested memories of specific North American events or North American people. "What we have here, then," he wrote in 1948, "is the saga of one of the oldest figures in Winnebago religion, probably the morning Star, whose deeds are . . . performed in an historical older period of Winnebago history . . . [but] a period about which . . . the author of the epic still possessed specific memories."[9]

The implications of Radin's thoughts are the same as those of Bob Salzer's belief that the particularities of the Gottschall artwork have a historical basis in the social upheaval and conflicts that resulted from Cahokia's big bang. For the history-minded analyst, both viewpoints mean that the intriguing details of the Red

Horn saga, the possibilities of a Mesoamerican link to the story, or any full explanation of Cahokia's big bang will not be possible based solely on an analysis of the narratives. For the full story, archaeologists must look to the materials and media of ritual commemoration and social action in the ground.

8

AMERICAN INDIAN ROYALTY

WITH ONE OR TWO POSSIBLE EXCEPTIONS, ridgetop mounds are found nowhere else in the world besides at Cahokia—where there are at least a dozen or so. These oddly shaped tumuli have narrow ridgelines running down their long axes, with sloping sides that meet at similarly angled and sloped ends. Though the French called them "earthen barns," they were probably intended to look more like palatial ancestral temples. Instead of temples' golden-yellow thatched roofs, though, the mounds featured dark-clay-hipped ridgetops, which signaled that these were resting places of the esteemed dead.

What makes the ridgetop mounds unique is their entombed and skeletonized human remains. No archaeologists have made similar finds or heard of such finds elsewhere. No European explorer, missionary, or wayfaring artist described or painted anything comparable. And no pre-Mississippian precedent has been found that can explain their origins or help interpret them.

Some additional archaeological information, however, is useful, even if it is spotty and anecdotal: Preston Holder and Joyce Wike's excavations into the Junkyard Mound, Warren King Moorehead's discovery in the Rattlesnake Mound, some details about the Powell Mound, and scattered tidbits in nineteenth-century newspaper accounts of the destruction of the St. Louis, East St. Louis, and Mitchell ridgetops. From these, archaeologists have drawn several observations.

First, most graves were laid on the surfaces of old flat-topped pyramids before being covered over with their new earthen ridgetop summits. So, as at Mound 72, the killings and other rituals performed on the summit stages were meant to be seen by all gathered below. It is also likely that an ancestral temple stood on the former surface or flat summit before being decommissioned and razed as part of the grand mortuary event, the ridgetop mound cap being added at the very end.

Second, the burials typically included mass interments of corpses in trenches or pits, as well as piled burials of skeletal parts. Sketchy details from the destroyed St. Louis, East St. Louis, and Mitchell ridgetop mounds suggest mass burials that were sometimes segregated by sex, which implies further sacrifices based on the evidence of mass burials of women at the fully excavated sites. But these mounds also contained piles of bones of a chosen few of the long dead, which had been saved for burial on such a significant occasion. In the Rattlesnake Mound, at the southern end of Cahokia, Moorehead's workers found rows of pile burials, like those in the Junkyard Mound and Mound 72, with multiple long bones or skulls of people grouped together as if gathered up from a charnel house, wrapped in shrouds or packed in baskets, and arranged on the mound surface. In several of the known cases, seashells and beads were heaped over the top of the multiple bodies or disarticulated bones.

Third, bodies of highly regarded people were interred in at

least some (and probably all) of the ridgetop mounds. This has been inferred from skeletal evidence and excavated artifacts, including copper ear ornaments, conch shells, arrowheads, a carved bird-effigy smoking pipe, shell-bead necklaces and beaded garments, and Cahokia-style chunkey stones. In at least two cases, the hoards of objects interred with the human remains included pots, stone axe heads (perhaps whole axes), and more beads. In one mound at Mitchell, sacred medicine bundles were found, consisting of copper objects, chipped-stone daggers, and imitation tortoiseshell rattles made from copper, all wrapped in rabbit skins. At least one crystal was discovered in the East St. Louis mound, reminiscent of the Mound 72 mica. In the St. Louis tumulus, a pair of little shield-shaped human-head earrings made from copper were found, suggesting a link to the narratives of the Iowa and Ho-Chunk.

All these artifacts are similar to those buried in Mound 72 or suggest some other aspect of the hero-twin stories that were painted on rock walls or retold by elders for generations. Bead-studded shrouds and beaded capes or blankets and the human-head earrings might have been associated with a Morning Star or Thunderbird impersonator or with twin-Thunderer burials. The other objects, particularly the beads, arrows, bird pipe, chunkey stones, and crystal, hint at a theatrical script like that followed in Mound 72. In two cases, beaded-cape burials were found at opposite ends of their mounds, hinting at the dualism seen in Mound 72. In a third case, at St. Louis's Big Mound, a pair of skeletons was found on an earlier summit; the larger of the two had been wearing copper human-head earrings.

The St. Louis mounds were destroyed before archaeologists had a chance to thoroughly document their contents, but existing reports give a general idea of what was found. According to one account, deep in the center of the Big Mound, a large wooden vault was discovered that was similar to the one Al Meyer recorded seeing in Mound 72's largest sacrificial pit.[1] Reportedly, it held twenty to thirty skeletons, buried with hundreds of white seashell beads. Two more such cedar-lined constructions were found in East St. Louis's thirty-nine-feet-high Cemetery Mound by workmen removing the great tumulus in 1870: Human "bones were found in two vaults . . . thirty feet below the [forty-foot-high] original apex of the mound." In one of the vaults, according to those who saw it, a limestone-slab roof rested on intact "wooden columns, and the sides were lined with wood; but all the woodwork had decayed, and the roof had fallen in, disarranging the bones, so that they appeared in confused heaps."[2]

John Kelly, an FAI-270 project veteran who excavated at the East St. Louis site in the early 1990s, believes that an 1870 newspaper reporter's description of the physical stature of the skeletons in this vault means that they were probably men. With them were piles of burial objects, including "jug-shaped vessels of unglazed earthenware, stone hammers, hatchets and chisels; oblong beads perforated in the center lengthwise, marine shells, arrowheads, vases, pieces of flint, etc." In the other pit, the reporter described a dozen smaller skeletons, which Kelly thinks were probably women.[3]

If these sacrificial victims were clubbed or strangled to death like those in Mound 72 or the Junkyard Mound, they were not the only such examples from Cahokia and East St. Louis. For instance, Warren Wittry found the severed arms and legs of four people, buried in a garbage pit next to a plaza post on Tract 15A. Another sacrificial victim associated with a post pit was found by University of Illinois archaeologists at the East St. Louis site in 2000. The skeleton of a young adult female was at the bottom of a very large post pit, nearly six feet deep. Her wrists and ankles appear to have been bound; after execution, her limp body had been tossed into the open hole where once a giant timber had stood. Finally, an old newspaper account tells of another East St. Louis mound, north of the Cemetery Mound, dug up by Anglo citizens in the 1870s. In it they found eighteen bodies arranged in a circular starburst pattern. The corpses had been carried to the burial site and laid with their heads pointed away from the circle's center and their feet pointed toward it. Many of the skulls had fractured temporal bones, presumably the result of being hit with a blunt instrument, reminiscent of the cases observed in the Mound 72 pits.

It is difficult to know if all such executions were carried out for the same reason, although the associations with either temple marker posts or ridgetop mounds suggest a relationship. Robert Hall thought that many of these deaths could be explained in the same way as were Mesoamerican and later Pawnee executions: as tribute to the Morning Star or Corn Mother.[4] That may well have been the case; however, this does not adequately explain all the findings.

There is some uncertainty about whether a few of the dozen or so ridgetop mounds were true ridgetop mounds. What the railroads and commercial interests did not tear down in the nineteenth and twentieth centuries, American farmers plowed repeatedly, season after season, for more than a century, causing the original shapes of the mounds to erode. Even more damaging was that shallowly buried tombs or bones were often ripped through by horse-drawn and later tractor-pulled steel plows. Even careful digging by expert archaeologists has sometimes failed to establish whether a mound was one of the unique ridgetop types or simply a heavily eroded and plowed-down platform mound.

In any event, at one time there were at least nine and perhaps as many as sixteen of these special tomb mounds. From the looks of their contents, and from the dated contents of Fowler's Mound 72 and Holder and Wike's Junkyard Mound, they were not all contemporaries, although all date within a two-century period, the late 1000s to early 1200s—the heyday of Cahokia. Mound 72 dates to the late 1000s, its sequential burials perhaps stretching into the early 1100s. The East St. Louis, Powell, and Junkyard mounds, and probably others, most likely were constructed in the 1100s. Finally, the Mitchell and perhaps St. Louis mounds date to the end of that span and possibly into the early 1200s.

The significance of this time span is that it covers approximately ten human generations of twenty years each. Thus, if these mounds were sequential constructions, as seems likely, then at least one ridgetop mound exists for every generation within Cahokia's century-and-a-half reign. Some archaeologists have speculated that the ridgetop mounds were simply the final resting places of people from a single lineage or clan, perhaps after they had lost power or influence. But another intriguing possibility exists. The ridgetop mounds, many occupying prominent, highly visible locations, may have been the inauguration mounds of living rulers—and therefore a principal means by which Cahokian society was integrated.

According to this argument, the mortuary theatrics on the mounds may have involved actors or impersonators who played specific parts in grand, staged plays that were intended to be seen and experienced by large audiences. That dramatic performances involved impersonators is known from several American Indian groups. For instance, certain individuals among the Siouan-speaking groups of the eastern Plains, including the Omaha, Osage, Hidatsa, and Mandan, impersonated one or both of the hero twins; an especially prominent individual called Honga impersonated the Ancient One. More to the point, around 1630 Father Gabriel Sagard witnessed a reincarnation ritual among the Iroquois that shared features with those probably played out in Cahokia's ridgetop theater. He wrote that after carrying in the bones of the dead chief, the actors

> all stand upright, except the one who is to raise the dead;
> on him they impose the name of the deceased, and all,
> placing their hands down low, feign to raise him back to

life in the person of this other man. The latter stands up, and after loud acclamations from the people he receives the gifts offered by those who were present, [and] who . . . thenceforth regard him as if he were the deceased person whom he represented.[5]

The power of such reincarnation rites should not be underestimated. Given the prominence and pomp of the ridgetop spectacles, the Cahokian events, which were unlike burial rites anywhere before or after, may have brought about something new—new to the agricultural folks of greater Cahokia, new to the Midwest and South, and new to the world.

Such a way of thinking about reincarnation rites—or any events, theatrical performances, material objects, human bones, or social actions generally—is relatively new to American archaeology, and not commonly accepted. By the 1970s and 1980s, American archaeology was undergoing a sea change. A wave of ecological theorizing was sweeping the field, and archaeologists were encouraged to shift their focus away from traditional theories of cultural history that sought to explain, however rudimentarily, cultural identities, technological diffusions, and migrations, among other things. Beginning in the 1960s, archaeologists began to think of themselves as scientists; humanistic approaches that emphasized individuals, ideologies, historical oddities, or unique cultures fell out of favor. In their place, evolutionary theories, which suggested that certain adaptive human behaviors would be selected over time, began to gain prominence. The resulting perspective, which was readily adopted by Cahokia and FAI-270 project archaeologists of the time, held that social change happened through the gradual evolution of native populations who adapted to their environments. Thus, the job of archaeologists boiled down to seeking the ecological reasons for whole-group adaptations. Less attention was focused on inequalities within populations, differential access to resources, and economic imbalances. For Cahokia studies, this meant a change in the way archaeologists viewed the religious, political, and economic relationships between the city and its outlying farmers.

Bareis and Porter and their FAI-270 project supervisors wrote reports that highlighted the locations, facilities, architecture, and dietary remains of the ancient people, which reflected the "adaptive strategies" of local Mississippian farmers. In the mid-1980s, Thomas Emerson, George Milner, John Kelly, Mark Mehrer, and other FAI-270 archaeologists posited that the farmsteads they were excavating around Cahokia produced direct, unequivocal evidence of an adaptive strategy wherein farmers maximized crop production as a natural, evolutionary consequence of an ever-growing population. These farmers were viewed as autonomous and subject to an evolutionary process separate from that of the elites who lived at Cahokia. Even Holder's and Fowler's ridgetop-mound discoveries were said to have been somehow typical of an elite mortuary behavior distinct from and unrelated to that of farmers.

Some archaeologists continue to believe that an ecological model best explains Cahokia's development into a megacenter. Even today, such people dislike terms such as "big bang" or "city" to describe Cahokia. Others, however, have moved back toward a humanistic cultural-historical approach. Emerson, for example, beginning in the late 1980s, was studying the symbolism of the red flintclay carvings and considering the possibility that Cahokia's leaders were directing farm production through ideology. By the early 1990s, the theoretical pendulum was swinging back toward concerns about inequality, domination, power, and cultural plurality. And about that same time, archaeologists began to return to the old digs of Holder, Wittry, Bareis, and Hall, which had never been systematically studied.

Examining the layout of houses and their domestic refuse from Wittry's dig at 15A established that the most dramatic changes—in how people made a living, how they built their houses, and what sorts of finery they possessed—occurred simultaneously around 1050. Evidence from the decades before the Woodhenge was built showed that the new and enlarged, post-1050 neighborhood on Tract 15A was segregated by status, with larger houses in the north (associated with another novel sort of building, a sweat lodge) and smaller ones in the south (without sweat lodges). But whether high or low status, everybody at Cahokia seemed to have had more craft objects and ritual paraphernalia than rural people, especially in the years immediately after 1050.

This insight—that there was inequality at New Cahokia and that some people might have benefited from the revolutionary changes more than others—opened up big possibilities, which were expanded by additional studies of two old excavations. The first was the author's own analysis of Preston Holder's diggings into a pyramid on the north side of the Cahokia site. Here, after he had found all the skeletons in the Junkyard Mound, Holder carefully salvaged sections of the Kunnemann platform mound, which had been slated for destruction for its fill dirt by the highway department. What he found there in 1955–56 surprised him: evidence of a carefully maintained monument that seemed to have been in a constant state of construction. Holder imagined what the mound-building project must have been like: "Little increments of fill and surfaces are continually being diddled with—put it up, take it down, clear it off, build something else, put in posts, take them out, dig trenches, and then refill them—all over the place." And this was the case "all the way through the mound."[6]

New examinations of his work and subsequent excavations of other Cahokia mounds suggest that Cahokian monumental constructions were all works in progress, just as Holder thought. Every year the pyramids were reconditioned, their buildings refurbished or completely removed. Afterward, workers brought in more earth to carefully resurface the mound, and the surmounting pole-and-thatch temples, houses, council buildings, and storage huts were then reconstructed. From the looks of things, the regular participation by many people in building and rebuilding these pyramid-summit architectural complexes was in and of itself a primary goal of monument building at Cahokia.

The second revelation came from the author's analysis of one of Charles Bareis's digs, possibly his most important. Besides working alongside the crew salvaging Cahokia and various outlying sites in the 1960s, Bareis also ran a field school, training University of Illinois students to dig. This he did quite thoroughly, from all reports, initially at what was left of Mound 51, which was being plundered for fill dirt to build the subdivision of sixty houses that would eventually cover a large part of the Grand Plaza. Besides the many layers of fill in Mound 51, like those seen in Holder's Kunnemann Mound, Bareis found something else beneath the mound: a giant refilled "borrow"—the gouged-out area from which earth had been taken to build the mounds or to level the plaza in the first few years of New Cahokia.

It appears that what is now called the "sub–Mound 51 borrow pit" had been dug alongside the newly built Grand Plaza sometime around 1050, probably to obtain the earth needed to level the plaza or build the lowest stage of Monks Mound. Originally this pit appears to have been more than 195 feet long, 62 feet wide, and, at its center, 10 feet deep. After the Cahokians dug this great gash into the earth, they refilled it over a period of a few years with the richest and rankest garbage imaginable in the ancient Cahokian world. When Bareis and his students finally reached one wet and deeply buried deposit deprived of oxygen all those years, they reeled back in disgust. The nine-hundred-year-old waste was remarkably preserved, if slowly rotting.

The organic and artifactual remains were arranged in a series of discrete layers representing a series of massive dumpings, burnings, and garbage burials. Each of the eight primary strata was a phenomenally rich, high-density mix of used and broken ritual objects, the latter including a chunkey stone, a smoking pipe, exotic arrowheads, an earspool, a seashell-bead necklace, quartz crystals, specially painted or decorated pots, and debris from the manufacture of special axe heads and woodworking tools. More common than these were the remains of the cooking and consumption of great amounts of food.

Thickly layered in the pit's strata were shards from thousands of broken cooking pots, bones of many thousands of deer and other animals, and seeds, fruits, and rinds left behind from the preparation of pumpkin and corn soups, corn bread, and gruels and porridges, as well as the remains of various nuts and berries. There were also burned parts of houses or temples, including one huge layer of old roof thatch, pieces of several human skeletons, cypress wood chips from the trimming or shaping of timbers or giant marker posts, cedar branches (perhaps from old brooms to ceremoniously sweep away this garbage), and, scattered throughout the fills, burned tobacco seeds. Based on the sheer density of excavated remains, individual feasts that took place over the course of just a few days would have involved killing, butchering, and carting in as many as thirty-nine hundred deer, the use of up to seventy-nine hundred pots, and enough smoking tobacco to produce more than a million charred tobacco seeds.[7]

That is enough food to feed a city and enough native tobacco—known for its high nicotine content—to give all smokers a hallucinogenic buzz. In other words, the sub–Mound 51 pit contained the remains of great Cahokian festivals, with invitees doubtless numbering in the thousands, possibly more than ten thousand. Given the religious objects, imagery, and residues of ceremony in the pit, one can presume that residents and visitors were treated to spectacular pomp and pageantry.

The deeper meanings and purposes of such grand gatherings may have been more complex and multifaceted than meets the eye.

After all, at roughly the same time these megafestivals were going on, during the decades after 1050, young women were being periodically sacrificed just several hundred yards south of the Grand Plaza at Mound 72. It is unclear whether the two kinds of events happened simultaneously or were kept separate.

In any case, the Cahokians seem to have been building a new kind of esprit de corps, a new sense of community—a community that, in its mix of festive gatherings and human sacrifice, in a way, linked church and state. Possibly Cahokians accommodated the bizarre mortuary spectacles and tolerated the excesses of their leaders in part because of social and economic rewards that might have accompanied the great festivals.

Looking back on the FAI-270 project excavations and other rural settlements dug since, Thomas Emerson now argues that the same abrupt transition evident in Wittry's Tract 15A dig was also apparent in the open countryside immediately surrounding Cahokia. That is, by 1050, the old villages and hamlets of ordinary people appear to have been swept away, and not by the Mississippi River, to be replaced, if at all, by single-family farmsteads. These farmsteads were, in turn, interspersed with strategically placed temples, sweat lodges, and the homes of high-status families. Emerson thought that the shift was abrupt, as if the rural folks were actually replaced by new people or select families from the population. This became known, informally, as the "replacement hypothesis," and it suggests something extraordinary: New Cahokia's transformation was, at its core, the confederation of a state government by means of some cultlike religious practices involving rulers' impersonating and making sacrifices to their ancestors and their gods.

Most anthropological theories posit that "the state" is a central government that controls labor in a way that supersedes kinship and community ties. Such governments, known in the ancient worlds of Mesopotamia, China, Mexico, and Peru, have sufficient authority to allocate or dispose of labor as they see fit. The rulers and administrators warehouse resources and stockpile foods for use in the state's projects. They "ruralize" a region's producers and encourage, through their political-economic activities, the stratification of society.[8] They also make the rules. And while not all of these outcomes have been proved beyond a doubt (see the next chapter), there are reasons to believe that such a state government was, at the very least, under production at New Cahokia beginning in 1050.

Some archaeologists suggest that the supernova of 1054 could have provided the pretext for a series of demonstrations—the more theatrical the better—of the legitimate power and authority centered in some person or small group of people. For the Cahokian governors, that theater seemed to take the form of a grand and repetitive retelling of the age-old story of human creation through festivals, chunkey matches, and mortuary rites. As we see most clearly in evidence from the ridgetop mounds, such a story featured both men and women, good and evil, light and dark, day and night, summer and winter, and the living and the dead. The leaders of New Cahokian society may have believed that if they could associate themselves with the source of life and death on earth—with creation itself—their rule would be unquestioned and unchallenged.

Thus the significance of the ancestral-temple rites, the large wooden marker posts, and the mortuary spectacles evidenced in Cahokia: The ridgetop mounds were great theatrical stages where supernatural forces were made manifest on earth, perhaps in the person of one or more living Cahokian rulers. The mortuary rites, conducted every few years, may have been the very means by which living heirs in a "royal" line of succession assumed their part in a new, or significantly revamped, grand supernatural narrative of creation on earth. Perhaps, as with the Iroquois, these living players would step into the scene through smoke and crystalline mirrors, or be carried to the stage with the dead, only to arise and walk away.

Such an elaborate narrative or Cahokian ideology was also culturally commemorated through the annual cycle of great ceremonious religious festivals, where all community members would come to eat, dance, play chunkey, pray, observe the play of light on the Woodhenge, work on the temples and pyramids, and smoke potent tobacco specially grown for the event. These were festivals of life, but they were also celebrations of death. So the findings of pieces of human skeletons in the mix of feasting debris under Mound 51—likely pieces of ancestors normally kept in temples—should not be viewed as odd.

Even female sacrifices, while taboo in some cultures, might have been considered culturally appropriate, or even in some way "normal," at Cahokia. According to the new standards of the day, female sacrifices were not merely one-off events associated with the death of rulers; they may have been the central events in Cahokia's grand ritual theater, performed every few years or whenever the stars, moon, or sun were in correct alignment. In the Junkyard Mound, there were no male interments similar to the beaded-blanket burial of Mound 72. Rather, it seems that the elaborate ceremony there, the death if not execution of two or more women—one during childbirth—and their children and dog, was associated with the termination of some ancestral lineage and the emptying out of that group's charnel house. In this case, the dead might have been from a rival faction whose own claims to Cahokian rulership were effectively struck down by whoever emerged alive from the dispute.

In Mound 72, one or two mass sacrifices of women preceded the deaths of the two men on and under the bead-studded thunderbird cape, seemingly buried to honor the ideas or forces represented by the giant wooden posts. Like the Omaha's Venerable Man, these posts quite possibly embodied the masculine ancestors of living rulers. And if the gendered sticks and stones of the chunkey game or the hoops and poles of its older variant are any clue, then the penetration of Mother Earth by ancestral male poles might have been considered a monumentally important cosmological balancing act.

In this light, the question of who the women sacrificed at Cahokia were takes on critical importance. These women told their side of the story, willingly or not, using the ultimate medium, their bodies. Possibly they were captives, taken from their hometowns in a practice similar to that of the Pawnee in the historical era. They might also have been considered slaves, as were captives recorded by French observers in the colonial American South. Or they might have been local farm girls who understood their part in a community-wide celebratory drama, as symbolic wives of the Morning Star or personifications of goddesses: Blood Woman, Xilonen, Red-Haired Giantess, or Girl-with-the-white-beaver-skin-as-a-wrap.

The identities of these sacrificed young women and their relationship to the larger narratives of pre-Columbian eastern North America have seldom been the focus of archaeological research. In part, this is because of a lack of guidance from recorded stories or rock-art storyboards like those at Picture Cave or the Gottschall Rockshelter that tell the Red Horn saga. This, in turn, may reflect a twentieth-century male bias in anthropology and archaeology: Anglo men tended to interview indigenous men (who tended to emphasize masculine themes and narratives), and ritual cave sites featuring masculine art tended to receive top billing in archaeological scenarios. As that bias receded, the importance of the feminine, agricultural side of the story began to emerge from the many large-scale digs around Cahokia.

The native accounts of the early Mississippians at New Cahokia were not merely inscribed on pots, painted on rock walls, or woven into a falcon-impersonator costume. In Warren Wittry's early digs at Tracts 15A and 15B, he found a huge red-painted wooden compound, a giant circular rotunda, and various reconstructions of an

American Woodhenge, all of which were, in effect, "monumental symbols," pieces of a giant storyboard written on the canvas of the entire region. The construction of such monuments—like four-sided earthen pyramids and plazas—made manifest an ordered understanding of a hierarchically structured, four-part universe, which divided the cosmos into the cardinal directions and was centered on Cahokia and mediated by Cahokians. Each of these collective constructions served as a social experience, which, given their standing walls and open interior spaces, continued to enable or constrain certain kinds of bodily movements, social gatherings, cultural associations, and storytelling for years thereafter.

Yet digging has also produced tangible evidence that has made archaeologists reevaluate the importance of women in Cahokian thinking. The later heirs of the Cahokia tradition of dirt archaeology in the American Midwest made discoveries that contextualize women and the participatory nature of cultural-narrative construction. Following Wittry's lead, Charles Bareis and James Porter had, by 1976, begun what would become the largest salvage-archaeology project ever undertaken in the United States: the FAI-270 Highway Mitigation Project. By the mid-1970s, federal laws were in place to prevent the wanton destruction of historical sites, so Bareis and Porter had an opportunity to fully fund the sort of extensive, mechanically aided excavations that they and Wittry had, with scarce resources, performed under emergency conditions in the 1960s. And while this time the highway planners did attempt to avoid the ancient site, their massive six-lane highway would inevitably destroy various Cahokian villages and farmsteads, including the BBB-Motor and Sponemann sites, on the very outskirts of Cahokia.

Both sites were parts of a larger village with a lone earthen pyramid, a little more than a mile northeast of Monks Mound.[9] Thomas Emerson and his assistant, Douglas Jackson, were in charge of the BBB-Motor dig, while Andrew Fortier, a former apprentice of Porter's, helmed the Sponemann excavation, also with Jackson's help. The BBB-Motor discovery came first. Emerson and Jackson were watching a huge earthmoving machine scrape the upper plow zones off the top of a small, natural floodplain ridge when it hit something hard and red. Jackson thought it was a piece of modern brick, but when he picked it up and rolled it over, a carved face stared back at him. It was the face of a woman, a goddess.

The find was a piece of an elaborately carved statuette, one of the red-stone objects now known to have been made at or near Cahokia out of soft flintclay from the nearby Missouri hills. It was the first of two statuettes found among the remains of a small temple that had stood at the site around the year 1100. Traces of similar temples were uncovered at the Sponemann site, a half mile away, at least one of which was built entirely out of red cedar and then ceremoniously burned down nine hundred years ago. On the floor beneath the burned timbers and collapsed roof thatch, archaeologists found pieces of four more charred temple statuettes, fragmented by the intense heat of the burning building.

All the Sponemann-site figure carvings show explicitly and naturalistically feminine attributes: curvilinear bodies, gracile facial features, and prominent breasts. All also appear to show some combination of snakes, baskets (presumed to contain ancestral bones), vines, and crops, hallmarks of a matronly goddess of fertility and ancestor worship. The first BBB-Motor carving shows the woman holding the handle of a garden hoe she had just dug deeply into the back of a great toothed serpent. The monster's tail then bifurcates and becomes two vines of squash plants or bottle gourds growing up the goddess's back. In another take on the same superhuman theme, one of the Sponemann statuettes shows the woman holding a gourd in each hand; the vines run up her back and, in wrapping around her head, become a serpent. In three more-fragmentary statuettes, two coiled serpents and female faces and bodies hold open or emerge from baskets.

The finds caused elation in the ranks of the FAI-270 project diggers, as they provided proof positive of the need to dig everything that remained of entire sites, as had been espoused by Holder, Wittry, and others. Rejoined for a time by Wittry himself, these archaeologists were rediscovering what he had amply demonstrated at 15A and 15B: The narratives of the ancient ones were not simply written on a pot, pecked into a rock, or retold to an ethnologist by a single shaman in one sitting. Multiple narratives were mapped onto or written into the landscape by many people. And there, at the edge of Cahokia, another story was becoming apparent, one with unambiguous feminine overtones whose component parts were clear: women, serpentine earth deities, ancestors, and crops. In these material objects there was a strong sense of the feminine narrative, scarcely noted by the male storytellers of the Ho-Chunk, Iowa, Hidatsa, Natchez, or Caddo, and not painted on the walls of the Gottschall Rockshelter or Picture Cave.

Thomas Emerson traced that story in the 1980s and 1990s, tracking down other red-stone carvings found in earlier years, and suggested that Cahokians were obsessed with the feminine and fertility symbolism. All the BBB-Motor and Sponemann finds were female. Most of the others known from the region, if sex was apparent, also seemed to be of women. But, as Emerson later realized, the scale of the Mississippian narrative might exceed the Cahokia region.

After he proved, with the help of the laserlike PIMA device, that all carved red-flintclay images were made at Cahokia, it also became immediately apparent that, with only one or two exceptions, the gendered, anthropomorphic Cahokian sculptures found far afield— at Spiro, Shiloh, and other Mississippian towns or cemeteries in Arkansas, Louisiana, Tennessee, and beyond—were depictions of men: a chunkey player here, a shamanic priest there; a naked warrior here, a male hero wearing human-head earrings there. Since all were made at Cahokia, Emerson wondered what accounted for the uneven distribution of the various gendered sculptures. Almost all of the female statuettes were goddess figurines, probably carvings of a motherly deity if not Corn Mother herself. Presumably, he has suggested, these were so important to the Cahokians that their sculpted images were not, and perhaps could not be, traded away. Clearly, whatever explained the transregional distribution of carved sculptures had happened at a scale much larger than any one place, one art object, one rock-art panel, or one narrative. The fact that few feminine red-flintclay carvings were removed from Cahokia in ancient times, combined with the abundance of masculine imagery at Spiro and elsewhere, seems to have contributed to an overemphasis, in archaeological explanations, on the masculine hero-twin story, with its principal characters Red Horn, Lodge Boy, Civilized Boy, Wild Boy, Spring Boy, Afterbirth Boy, Thrown-Away, and the Thunderers depicted by classic Braden images of falcon impersonators, among other things.

In many ways, the situation was similar to the King-Tut-at-Spiro and Danzantes-at-Monte-Albán stories described in the first chapter: The clues left behind told a story that its tellers wanted to emphasize but that may not have corresponded exactly with the facts of their existence. But the finds of goddess sculptures in the burned temples near Cahokia attest to a more complex and large-scale truth. The heroic stories of the ancient past involved men and women, the feminine Evening Star and Corn Mother being as important as the masculine Morning Star. Moorehead had barely glimpsed this more complex truth. Holder and Wike had looked the graphic evidence of it full in the face but were left befuddled. And Melvin Fowler, having completely exposed its ghastly mortuary expression, was overwhelmed by its complexity.

However, in 1995, another discovery would further weaken the predominance of a male-oriented reading of Cahokian history.

New excavations at agricultural villages revealed that the feminine side of the story, the economic foundations of Cahokia, and the whole history of the larger Mississippian world were entangled in a web of relationships attached not just to the powerful rulers but, more important, to ordinary farmers.

9

DIGGING FOR THE GODDESS

IT ALMOST DIDN'T HAPPEN: a textbook piece of salvage archaeology that would change everything previously thought about Cahokia's mortuary theater, pre-Columbian history, and the explosion of Mississipian culture. And like the diggers of Mound 72, the archaeologists knew from the beginning that they had found something unexpected.

The discovery was made out on the edge of the Illinois prairie, a day's walk from Cahokia, during an old-fashioned salvage dig at one of the largest and most important early-Cahokian-era agricultural villages ever found. Called the Halliday site, it was ten miles southeast of Cahokia in a moderately rolling upland area that, by the mid-1990s, was rapidly becoming swamped by shopping malls and suburban housing developments.

Upland Mississippian farming settlements at the edges of southwestern Illinois's vast interior prairie were not unknown, but they were thought to have been largely irrelevant oddities. James

Griffin had recorded several prairie-edge Cahokian farming settlements in the 1940s after local artifact collectors had pointed them out. In the 1960s Robert Hall had trenched into a sizeable pyramid at one, and Chuck Bareis had excavated farmhouses at others during his highway salvage work. Clearly, there were farmers living in the hinterlands within two or three days' walk of New Cahokia, but archaeologists knew little more than that.

For a long time, studying the upland farmers was not a priority in Cahokia research. From a 1970s and 1980s point of view, explaining Mississippians meant focusing on the ways in which farmers had adapted to floodplains. The notion that environment caused culture change was so ingrained that, as recently as 2001, a prominent FAI-270 veteran could declare: "Nothing will be learned about Cahokia by looking in the uplands."[1] Still, in 1995, archaeologists driving through the area happened onto the partially bulldozed Halliday site and, to their shock, found the remains of numerous ancient houses in the middle of a construction site that would soon be transformed into a modern housing subdivision. Earlier that day, they had met with a local man who had been finding artifacts on the site. Reporting that just that morning he had found a most unusual rock, he retrieved it from his kitchen sink, where, to his wife's chagrin, he had washed it clean instead of doing the dishes. The archaeologists gasped when they saw it. It was a broken smoking pipe with carvings of a frog's face, a snake, and a human head.

Down at the construction site where the pipe was found, they quickly discovered the remains of a dozen pre-Columbian houses—neatly stripped of plow zone and fully exposed to the world—at the south end of what had been a much larger, nine-century-old village. According to later estimates, there had been 150 houses and storage sheds at the Halliday village, home to some two hundred to three hundred people when first settled, at or just before 1050. If not for the archaeologists' serendipitous drive-by, all traces of these ancient homes would have been scooped away when the workmen gouged out holes for the concrete basements to follow. But with the prodding of local concerned citizens, the state stopped the development.

The ensuing salvage-archaeology dig by archaeologists and students from universities in Illinois, New York, and Oklahoma lasted five years and resulted in the total excavation of the remains of several dozen ancient houses and their associated dense middens full of early-Cahokian-era trash. But something new and unexpected was also found. The ancient village of Halliday was anything but normal. For one thing, the house and pottery styles appeared either old-fashioned or foreign to the region. For another, the team was finding almost no male-associated artifacts. Instead, they found bone weaving tools, spindle whorls (for spinning fibers into yarn), and ample evidence of intensive farming, pot making, and communal cooking. But there were none of the typical arrowheads and no evidence of large game animals. In the trash, there was scarcely a bone from anything larger than a dog.

The trash itself was impressive, in both amount and type. It littered the living areas of the village, a clear contrast with the tidy Cahokians, known among archaeologists for their clean houses and spotless public spaces. And among the bits of trash was scarcely a single Cahokia-made ritual object, religious icon, or other object, not counting baked-clay disks and chunkey stones (of which there were quite a few). There was, however, abundant evidence of a diet abnormal for Cahokia and the Mississippi floodplain: The usual mix of fish, waterfowl, and deer was missing. These upland villagers, living at the edge of the Illinois prairie, were eating small lizards, frogs, snakes, turtles, and rodents, as well as large amounts of corn, possibly more than anybody else in the area at the time—probably cooked as soup, judging from the residues found in pots. They were also eating their dogs, which was not a common practice at Cahokia.

Upon closer inspection, it appeared that many of the ancient, broken cook pots from this site had not been made according to local Native American stylistic conventions. In fact, they closely resembled a tenth-century type of pot called Varney Red Filmed, made in southern Missouri, more than two hundred miles down the Mississippi River. Archaeologists today associate Varney pottery with the people of southeastern Missouri and northeastern Arkansas of a millennium ago. Nevertheless, these particular nonlocal-style vessels were made at the Halliday site, as has been proved by collecting the local clays and making replicas of the ancient pots and chunkey stones. In other words, it wasn't that the Varney pots were foreign; the Varney potters living at Halliday probably were. They were immigrants, or the children of immigrants, from southeastern Missouri or northeastern Arkansas, and they were heavily into chunkey.[2]

The Halliday residents weren't alone in the uplands. Many more contemporaneous villages, farmsteads, and special-purpose temple sites have since been located all over the area. Comparing the pot styles of some of these sites with those of the Halliday village excavations over the succeeding years, archaeologist Susan Alt concluded that large numbers of foreigners had been pulled into Cahokia's orbit, including people from southern Indiana. Some of these ancient immigrants appear to have settled at one or another of the upland villages in this rural farming zone east of Cahokia.[3] And most of them possessed, or had access to, chunkey stones.

On the basis of Alt's analysis of spindle whorls and the discovery of high densities of broken stone hoe blades, archaeologists are pretty certain that the immigrants were living in this upland zone for good reasons, at least good for Cahokia.[4] They were there to farm and to weave, probably compelled to produce a surplus that could be collected by Cahokians. That they did this at the behest of Cahokians seems clear from what happened to them later: Beginning about 1150, most of the descendants of the upland farmers left their farms for destinations unknown. There are few to no archaeological sites known from the upland zone in question dating to the late twelfth century on. Cahokia went into a political and economic tailspin beginning at about the same time.

Given the upland farmers' meager diet and marginal lifestyle, compared with those of Cahokians or other townspeople in the Mississippi River bottoms closer to the city, it is apparent that they had experienced the closest thing to a peasant lifestyle that had ever existed in pre-Columbian North America. They ate more corn and less protein than is healthy for a person. What protein they did eat was far from choice bits of meat, and the existence of these near-peasant farmers was far from ideal, even for the time. When they left the uplands just a century after their grandparents or great-grandparents had arrived, they vacated the region entirely. It is not certain where the émigrés went, but the possibilities include their ancestral homelands in and around Missouri's Bootheel and up the Ohio River to southern Indiana. As a point of comparison, recent studies of ancestral Puebloan migrations in the American Southwest agree that ancient agricultural people tended to move to places where they already had social connections or kin. For outward-bound farmers formerly associated with Cahokia, returning to the legendary lands of old Toltec or Varney villages might have made sense.

It may be no coincidence, then, that a series of Mississippian towns popped up south of Thebes Gap in the late twelfth century. They were smallish burgs by Cahokian standards, none covering more than fifty acres, the size of Cahokia's principal plaza. But their pots, possessions, and earthen pyramids look as if they are derived from or inspired by Cahokia.

If some or all of the Cahokian émigrés went into the Missouri Bootheel, they did not stay very long: By 1400, everybody who had lived there had also left. That is, all the towns that grew up around

1200, as well as their rural hinterlands in the Bootheel and contiguous regions, were totally abandoned. As a consequence, a vast unpopulated landscape—which archaeologist Stephen Williams has called "the Vacant Quarter"—was opened up from Cahokia in the north, emptied by 1350 or so, to near Memphis, Tennessee, in the south, vacated around 1400.[5]

Where the Mississippian émigrés went next is a pressing question, since that location might provide the missing link to the answer of who the Cahokians and their neighbors became. There are hints at some of the southeastern Missouri sites, most obviously in the form of red-stone smoking pipes (made of Catlinite from Minnesota), that the Bootheel Mississippians had been in some ways connected to people living nearer the Plains. On the basis of sixteenth-century Hernando de Soto expedition accounts and knowledge of where the Dhegiha-Siouan (including the Quapaw and Osage) and Caddoan (including the Pawnee) peoples lived in the colonial period, it is reasonable to suspect that some emigrating Bootheel peoples might have moved either south, into Arkansas; northwest, across the Ozark Mountains and up the Missouri River into the eastern Plains; or both.

However, it is in no way clear who Cahokia's descendants are, and it seems unlikely that there would be only one such descendant community. For starters, many peoples seem to have been pulled into early Cahokia, and it is possible that they splintered in as many different directions. In fact, the complex linguistic landscape of the lower Mississippi valley at first European contact makes it just as likely that many Cahokians, who had established twelfth- and thirteenth-century alliances or colonies in lands as far away as what is now Mississippi, might have traveled quite far to the south. Isolated Siouan-speaking groups, in fact, were encountered by early Europeans all the way down to the Gulf of Mexico. Moreover, given the prevalence of historic-era multiethnic and polyglot communities, it is also likely that Cahokian descendants joined up with non-Cahokians during their exodus. In the end, there may have been no pure Cahokian descendant group left. The diaspora might have produced none, or all, of the peoples known today by the various Siouan, Caddoan, and Algonkian tribal identities.

Wherever they went, and whoever they became, the Cahokians' migration history is still key to figuring out the process by which civilizations collapse and how that process is related to later indigenous nations encountered by Euroamerican traders, explorers, and envoys. Not many unconnected dots remain over the four centuries or so between the chunkey-playing Siouan and Caddoan peoples encountered by Hernando de Soto, Lewis and Clark, or Catlin and the Mississippians south of Thebes Gap. Nor are there many more missing links between the Mississippians who vacated the Bootheel by 1400 and those who lived upriver at eleventh- and twelfth-century Cahokia.

Although archaeologists are unable to connect those dots, given present data and the complexity of the likely fissions and fusions of populations in the intervening centuries, evidence strongly suggests that migrations, multiethnic communities, and the agriculture of nonelite men and women are the key factors that shaped the history of pre-Columbian middle America. The first migration leading up to the big bang occurred when certain families moved from their southern and eastern homes northward and westward, to the edge of a prairie near a city hundreds of miles away. Later migrations witnessed Cahokian farmers moving away and were followed, centuries later, by the evacuation of the entire central Mississippi valley. At a minimum, this indicates such a complex history of cause and effect that no single explanation of Mississippian farmers, cultural development, political evolution, or ecological adaptation suffices. The reasons for the rise and fall of particular Mississippian societies in different places and at various times varied depending on what farmers did. The evidence for migration and abandonment also suggests that, like later townspeople and administrators,

Cahokia needed those upland farmers, the ones whose subsequent departure then seems to have correlated with Cahokia's demise and the simultaneous growth of the Bootheel towns.

In this sense, the history of Cahokia and the subsequent spread of its people across North America rest with the farmers: their labor power, their identities, and their unofficial histories. Cahokia researchers, many trained in the 1970s and 1980s, are not always united in their opinion of the history-making potential of these low-status people, their crafts, artwork, burial practices, and participation in public performances and building projects. The argument tends to hinge on population estimates and often on assumptions that ecology-minded Indians would never have lived in a densely packed city. Using low population estimates of Cahokia and its hinterlands, some archaeologists argue that farmers weren't really needed by Cahokians, and vice versa. This school of thinking downplays the effort required for building mounds and suggests that a large population wasn't necessary to explain their construction.

Yet there is also evidence to argue that, from Cahokia's beginning, its construction projects were larger than earlier archaeologists had estimated, and that Cahokia's organization, schedule, and design necessitated a substantial, well-orchestrated labor force. For instance, the entire central complex—including the fifty-acre plaza, the initial twenty-foot stage of Monks Mound, and the clay cores of all the other central mounds—was built in a huge, one-time labor project around 1050. It might have been the largest urban-renewal project ever undertaken at Cahokia, but there were others. Teams of researchers have found evidence that supports the notion of a series of massive urban-renewal projects at Cahokia and East St. Louis.

The first such demonstration was made by archaeologists Rinita Dalan and George Holley in the 1980s. They used special magnetic and electrical "geophysical" devices that could detect construction fill and the remains of houses and pits without having to excavate; using these devices, they discovered that the Grand Plaza was, in fact, an artificially leveled and layered feature.[6] Verifying their hypothesis with small-scale excavations, they proved that there were artificially buried natural ridges and fill-in swales under the plaza. It was apparent that the builders of the plaza had truncated the ridgetops and used the dirt to fill and level adjacent low-lying swales. They probably also used some of the dirt fill to help build the new pyramids, which were under construction at the time.

In 1997, another team, including Susan Alt and Jeff Kruchten, excavated in this same area in advance of a water main planned to cut across Cahokia's Grand Plaza, opening up a T-shaped trench seven-tenths of a mile long that would expose, for the first time, the entire length and breadth of the plaza. It was a challenging dig, in part because it took twenty minutes to walk from one end to the other. What the team found at Cahokia that summer confirmed Dalan and Holley's earlier model: The flat central feature of downtown Cahokia was an artificial landform. In portions of the waterline trench as well as under a small ridgetop mound in the middle of the plaza, the original land surface of Old Cahokia was discovered, buried by plaza fill. Alt and Kruchten also documented the truncated natural ridges and artificially filled-in areas that dated to about 1050. Finally, they observed that most of the plaza's fifty-acre cut-and-filled surface had subsequently been blanketed by a foot-thick layer of yellowish sandy silt, reminiscent of construction layers in a Cahokian pyramid.

This strongly suggests that the plaza was a single construction effort at the very inception of the city, not a multicentury project. Thus, its construction would have involved every able-bodied adult from the thousand-plus people living at Cahokia around 1050, and probably hundreds to thousands more from allied communities. Even then, digging, hauling, and dumping all that dirt might have taken weeks if not months. There would also have been hard-to-quantify investments in ceremony, in the form of feasts and celebrations, for this and all subsequent labor projects. In order to understand the apparent spontaneity of the giant convergence of people at New Cahokia in the middle of the eleventh century, it is imperative to look at how labor was organized and, not incidentally, who the laborers were.

Just to host a feast the size of those documented in the immense refilled sub–Mound 51 borrow pit excavated by Charles Bareis necessitated a large, readily available food surplus and an easily mobilized labor force. While some archaeologists believe that ecology-minded American Indians produced only what was needed to survive, the evidence is consistent with a model positing that Cahokian production aimed at producing not the minimum but the maximum. Enough surplus food and labor would have been needed to stage grand theatrical performances and to host enormous feasts with hundreds to thousands of guests. Cahokians would have needed to fill their storehouses in advance to ensure their collective future, to attract workers, to reward craftspeople or collaborators, and to feed the people in times of need and at celebrations.

Cahokia's economy was doubtless subject to unpredictable crop production and producer allegiance, and like many civilizations, Cahokia was almost certainly affected by political machinations that threatened to shift the power balance. This doubtless helps to explain the Junkyard Mound women and children, the thirty-nine clubbed people lying in the lower level of the Mound 72 pit (Feature 229), and possibly other ridgetop mortuary theatrics. With sacrifices, leaders could eliminate some rival claimants to office, impress the viewing public, and reaffirm the balance of the cosmos all at once.

Additional evidence of this was found by accident in 1992, when the Illinois Department of Transportation funded excavations at the East St. Louis site. Not long after Brackenridge had passed through in 1811, Anglo-Americans had founded a town on the same site, grading down or carting off the earth contained in the forty-five mounds at this ancient Cahokian suburb. The largest one, the ridgetop Cemetery Mound, was looted and razed in 1870, as recorded in the newspaper accounts noted earlier. With that, archaeologists long assumed that the entire site had been obliterated. But it had not.

Working on the south and north sides of Interstate Highway 55-70, archaeologists Andrew Fortier, Fred Finney, Don Booth, and John Kelly and their highway-project crews found the wall foundations of scores of elite houses, giant post pits, the basal layers of the razed mounds, and a vertical-post palisade wall buried intact beneath modern rubble. They also stumbled into the middle of a kind of miniature Pompeii. A large portion of the East St. Louis site, sometime around 1160, had been burned to the ground in some catastrophic or commemorative conflagration. Archaeologists have surmised, based on additional burned remains found north of the interstate in later excavations, that the fire destroyed several houses and temples and upwards of fifty small storage houses, huts, or granaries within an elaborate elite compound. The dozen-plus storage huts excavated contained a full complement of domestic tools, chipped-stone knife and hoe blades, stone axe heads, and fancy ceramic pots, baskets, and wooden bowls, some full of shelled maize.

Circumstantial evidence from excavations beneath the former location of the Cemetery Mound, near this compound, suggests that its two mortuary vaults were sealed and mounded over sometime late in the twelfth century. Thus, it is possible that the mortuary ceremony surrounding the burial of small and large skeletons, piles of interred objects, and an individual on a beaded cape also entailed the ritual burning of the complex. But it is also possible that some enemy of the East St. Louis elite somehow managed to penetrate the inner defenses, igniting the thatched roofs of the large, closely spaced buildings inside the walls, forcing the residents of the compound to flee as their homes and storage huts burned. Either cause seems to imply that the political stakes of the time were high indeed.

Evidence of a similar sort of elite compound, albeit unwalled, was found out in the rural upland hinterlands at a site originally identified by Thomas Emerson's highway archaeologists. Excavating ahead of heavy development in the area in 2001–2, Alt and Kruchten discovered a unique hilltop site, called Grossmann after the owner, that had been occupied by Cahokian elites, near villages occupied by immigrant farmers (such as Halliday). Alt, Kruchten, and a bevy of student archaeologists and volunteers stripped the disturbed plow zone from what remained of the site and then excavated the remains of nearly one hundred houses or house reconstructions. In so doing, the team documented that the houses were rigidly aligned and packed onto the hilltop. The archaeologists also saw something they had not seen before at a farming village: council houses. There were four of them, and they were as big as those previously found at East St. Louis, Cahokia, and Mitchell.

But the biggest surprise came afterward, as one field-school student began scraping aimlessly at the dirt near the house floor he had been assigned to excavate. He hit a rock, a big one. Soon he hit another rock, then more. He had found a cache of buried groundstone axe heads. As the student dug on, he found eight, twelve, twenty, and still more. All of them were wedged into a small pit next to a house and near the entrance to a council house. The one he had hit first was the largest and was intentionally laid atop those beneath. It later weighed in at twenty pounds and measured twenty inches in length, the largest stone axe head ever recovered from such a context by an archaeologist. The team worked on into the evening and, by nightfall, had mapped, photographed, numbered, and removed seventy axe heads in what *Archaeology* magazine called a "cold hard cache."[7]

Back in the lab the following autumn, Alt laid out the objects, which filled a long table. After some mixing and matching, a series of types began to emerge: Some were long, some short, some fat, some narrow; some were made from greenish rock, and others were bluish, black, or speckled with white phenocrysts. When she compared them to the map of the pit, Alt realized that the axe heads had, in fact, been buried as discrete sets. Most sets seem to have been pairs laid into the hole together. Other sets comprised more than two axe heads. The largest set contained more than a dozen, of a variety later determined to have been made at Cahokia.

Alt suspected that people, probably farm families from the surrounding villages, had gathered at this special hilltop site in the middle of the upland farming district to hold council and then to literally "bury the hatchets." Judging by the configuration of the objects, each person or family took a turn in laying axe heads into the pit. The biggest donor, perhaps suitably, was someone who possessed the Cahokia-variety hatchets. Like public ceremonies today that open with the pledge of allegiance, the ancient American ceremony may have somehow conveyed the sense that the people were united. The sentiment might have been repeated on other occasions, as there are several other axe-head burials known from key sites in the region.

There may also have been other, similar ceremonial events at which more than just possessions were at stake. A gathering of multiple farm families and Cahokians to bury axe heads is one sort of communal event. So is a gathering of people to build earthen and wooden monuments. Likewise, laying axe heads into a pit at a rural site is not so different from contributing piles of chunkey stones or bundles of arrows to the staged mortuary events at Cahokia. To stretch the analogy even further, the burying of inanimate objects by farm families could be likened to the sacrificial interment of the daughters of families from these or other farming villages. The largest of the seventy axe heads might even be comparable to the "matron" among the fifty-three women in Mound 72. It is a stretch, but the bodies in the ridgetop mounds might have been used as props to tell a story of creation and rebirth at Cahokia, just as the structured deposition of axe heads in the hinterlands told a story of a new esprit de corps between farmers and Cahokians. In fact, the connection between upland farmers and sacrificial rites could be stronger than one might think at first glance and, thus, the history of the entire interior of North America might, in a way, be connected to the story of those women, the history of Cahokia's upland farmers, and the great Corn Mother goddess of ancient America.

This line of thinking leads back to the discovery of the low-status women who lived at the Halliday site. Perhaps the Cahokian practice of sacrificing women was designed to minimize the impact on the lives of loyal local followers, who might not cotton to having their nubile women sacrificed. Thus, perhaps Cahokians captured women from distant groups (as the Pawnee did) or expected them as tribute from some less-connected marginal population (such as the immigrants in the upland farming villages). Being of different ethnic or status backgrounds, such foreign or marginal people might have had a different diet than Cahokians, who ate well. Last, given the importance of the ridgetop-mound rituals, the persons therein, and the grand narrative being constructed, the women to be sacrificed might have been in some way desirable for the purpose intended.

A puzzle piece linking Cahokia's elaborate mortuary mounds and the upland farmers falls into place once the physical characteristics of the sacrificed women in Mound 72 are taken into account. These women stand out markedly from the other Cahokians interred there in several ways. After studying the heritable traits of the various skeletons, along with indicators of disease and trauma, Jerome Rose concluded that there was little doubt that some of those killed were not from the city. First, the dental morphology of the sacrificed women's teeth, a heritable trait, was different from that of the rest of the status burials in the mound. Second, these women had a high rate of hyperostosis (a bone disease stemming from iron deficiency), which is typically a function of a poor diet. They also had more cavities on average, compared to others buried in Mound 72 and elsewhere, indicative of a high-carbohydrate diet. Finally, they had a lower-than-normal rate of periostitis, another bone disease, characterized by an inflammation of the soft tissue—mostly of the lower legs. Rose reasoned that, while the sacrificed women weren't particularly healthy, they would have had fewer skin imperfections or leg inflammations than other women. That is, they may have been chosen for sacrifice because of their good looks.

Another strong piece of evidence comes from bioarchaeologists Jane Buikstra and Stan Ambrose, who have done isotopic studies of the bones from Mound 72 to determine whether the diets of the high- and low-status men and women buried there were the same or different.[8] Some plants, especially maize, leave distinctive and detectable signatures in human bones. Analysts who carefully measure the quantities of carbon isotopes can tell how much corn an individual has eaten. The same is true of nitrogen isotopes, which accumulate in the bones if one eats meat. Buikstra and Ambrose measured these quantities in the bones and, compared to the nitrogen-rich diets of the high-status burials in Mound 72, those of the sacrificed women in the various pits consisted of less meat and more maize.

At first glance, this seems like a logical conclusion. The women lived at a time when maize was a staple crop. The belief in a Corn Mother goddess would seem to confirm that. However, both anthropologists and World Health Organization officials know that too much maize, to the exclusion of other foods, is detrimental to one's health. Famous studies link the substitution of maize for rice in Africa and the American South with a severe deterioration in human health. Corn, as it turns out, is missing a vital amino acid present in rice, meats, and other grains.

By this measure, the sacrificed women were not, as a group, eating as well as the average high-status Cahokian, who ate less corn and more meat. Moreover, sacrificed women were probably drawn from a distinct nonlocal population, given their dental characteristics. Finally, they may have been selected for their lack of skin imperfections—which is to say, their beauty. Women's bodies seem to have been a readily available commodity, appropriated from time to time for the ultimate sacrifice. But the question remains who might have been chosen for sacrifice.

At Cahokia, high-status local women might be ruled out as likely sacrificial victims, unless they were from families whose bloodlines were selected for elimination because they posed a threat to the royal families. Such a ritual elimination might explain the high-status women and children in the Junkyard Mound. Moreover, among indigenous North Americans during the historical period, captive women were often the logical choice for sacrifice. The Pawnee Morning Star ceremony typically involved one young female from outside the local community.

Of course, in the Cahokia case, there were a series of other marginal bloodlines that might have been likely candidates for Cahokia's mortuary theater. The lowest-status farmers eating the most corn in the region were immigrants from the upland hinterlands. They were the closest, spatially, to Cahokia and yet the most distantly related and marginally connected population. They were immigrants, and archaeologists had discovered their unusual villages and ample evidence of "women's artifacts" by happenstance at Halliday in 1995. Students and supervisors had toiled for several years to salvage what they could, because there was a sense that the archaeological remains of these people might say something meaningful about Cahokia. Today, it seems that these upland farmers were entangled in a truly complex, centuries-old social history of labor, migration, politics, violence, and religion that links them to Cahokia and, ultimately, to the peoples known to later European and American explorers and ethnologists. In another way, as the next chapter will examine, that history may also link them to the great civilizations of Mesoamerica.

10

WRESTLING WITH THE GODS

IN THE PRERADIOCARBON ARCHAEOLOGY of 1930s and 1940s North America, archaeologists like James Griffin believed that the introduction of maize, a Mesoamerican crop, must have been an event of singular historical importance. The preliminary results from the large-scale New Deal excavations, mostly conducted under the aegis of Roosevelt's Works Progress Administration, seemed to suggest that corn, four-sided earthen pyramids, and Mississippian iconography had been adopted from Mexico as a package deal. Thus, Griffin and others believed that although "the sum total of traits that may have had a Mesoamerican origin is not great, they undoubtedly were of great importance in the formation of Mississippi[an] culture."[1]

Griffin and his contemporaries came up with a series of possible explanations for how Mesoamerican traits might have diffused into Mississippian-period North America. Antonio Waring, a prominent avocational archaeologist, and Preston Holder summarized the prevailing view in the 1940s:

The temple mound, the bird-serpent composite, the Hand and Eye, the human head held by the hair, the ceremonial hafted celt [axe] and possibly the Baton [mace or dagger] all have close counterparts in the Mixteca-Puebla "culture." . . . Since none of these Mexicanoid elements appear in the earlier Southeastern levels and since they arrive in a body, suddenly and late, it seems most likely that they are of Mexican origin. . . . Since diffusion from the Southwest, from the West Indies or from the North cannot be demonstrated, it seems inescapable . . . that the route of ingress lay along the Texas Coast. . . . Because of the nature of the complex and because of the fact that its spread seems to be to a great degree linked to the movements of Middle Mississippian groups, we feel that the spread of the complex from a single Southeastern community [or] group of communities is strongly suggested.[2]

The Texas coast, of course, is a natural corridor that connects Mexico with the Caddoan-speaking people at places such as Spiro, Oklahoma, in the north. Perhaps, some argued, central Mexicans had sent traders—what the Aztec would later call *pochtecas*—into the north. As late as the 1970s, James Porter thought that Mexican influences had moved north through the Caddoan area of Texas and Oklahoma, cutting through the Ozarks and over to the Mississippi River—a virtual riverine highway—and continuing up into the Mississippi floodplain and on to Cahokia.

But traders would be likely to bring goods, and no Mississippian archaeologist had found any. In fact, by 1990, Griffin—who had seen more sites in eastern North America than anybody else alive—had yet to find a single Mesoamerican artifact at any of them. In addition, more recent studies and a litany of new radiocarbon assays clearly established that Mesoamerican-looking four-sided pyramids of the Mississippian world were not the result

of a single influence point from Mesoamerica. Rather, such platform mounds were of great antiquity in North America. Archaeologists dated especially large and obvious examples in the South
to the Middle Woodland era (200 BCE to 400 CE). Mound building itself dates back fifty-five hundred years in Louisiana, making
it the oldest known monumental architecture in the New World.
These days, southeastern archaeologists joke that New World
civilization began in Louisiana and was later transplanted into
Mexico.

Other important facts complicate the Mesoamerican-import
story. Thanks to new radiocarbon dates, archaeologists know that,
while corn was domesticated in Mexico, it first appeared in eastern
North America around 200, though it was not cultivated very inten-
sively until after 800. Mississippian art styles, on the other hand, didn't
exist as such until after 1050, reaching their "fullest expression," according to art analyst and archaeologist James Brown, after 1250. In
short, maize, mounds, and Mississippians weren't a package deal.
Indeed, so completely decoupled are they today that most archaeologists concur with a position voiced in 2005 by Brown: "Mound-
building and chiefly organization as well as other social and
political characteristics at one time attributed to contributions from
tropical America no longer carry persuasion," he asserted. "This is
not to say that beliefs and practices of a stylistic sort have not circulated across the continents, but such patterns are significant on a
wholly different level from the forms of organization grown locally."[3]

Most archaeologists now believe that the Mississippian phenomenon as it emanated from Cahokia and its sister complexes was
homegrown, and today's international border seems to have been
an ancient boundary as well, stopping all but "beliefs and practices
of a stylistic [aesthetic] sort." This is similar to Robert Hall's explanations for why there are so many North American–Mesoamerican
similarities. "As impressive as the cosmologies of Mesoamerica were,"

Hall concludes, "they nevertheless emerged from a background ultimately once shared by all Native Americans of their day, often cross-fertilized as ideas diffused from area to area."[4] Hall believed that this general diffusion was central, rather than incidental, to North American cultural history, suggesting a need to understand the history of the connections between distant peoples in order to understand the true relationship between Mesoamerican and Mississippian civilizations.

Typically, the dismissal of Mesoamerican connections is rationalized among archaeologists by citing the environment. The eastern Woodlands, after all, stop in central Texas, and the Mississippians were, from a theoretical vantage point, "adapted" to the eastern Woodlands. Therefore, it seems to follow logically that the later pre-Columbian peoples of the eastern United States would not have left the Woodlands to venture south into a barren and supposedly inhospitable land of sagebrush and sand. There was six hundred miles of semiarid brushland and a sandy coastline between the Woodlands and Mesoamerica.

That distance, however, would have been more easily traversed in boats along the coast. Archaeologist Nancy White believes that Mexicans, if not also their Caribbean cousins, might have journeyed north, intentionally or not, just by floating on the currents of the Gulf of Mexico.[5] Such water travel would not have been unusual; Cahokians, after all, probably traveled hundreds of miles up the Mississippi and Missouri rivers to trade, raid, or convert the peoples in those places on a semiregular basis.

Indeed, most archaeologists have no trouble accepting that native midwestern people paddled twelve hundred miles up into Yellowstone two millennia ago to extract obsidian, a prized black volcanic glass from which artisans chipped elaborate ceremonial knives. Ancient Louisianans, some thirty-five hundred years ago, repeatedly traveled hundreds of miles between Poverty Point and the south Appalachians, the Ozarks, and the southern Piedmont.

And, of course, the earliest people on the continent, Paleo-Indians, routinely traveled great distances on foot.

Still, many archaeologists are hesitant to prioritize the importance of Mesoamerican influence on Mississippian culture, ostensibly because of distance. One exception is Alice Kehoe, who has believed for a long time that there are a host of possible Mesoamerican-inspired objects, costumes, monuments, and linguistic features among North America's indigenous peoples. And among these she still lists rectangular pyramid-and-plaza complexes, which are, after all, more than mounds and can probably be dated back to the Classic period in Mexico, the equivalent of the so-called Middle and Late Woodland period in the lower Mississippi valley. A particularly good example of a North American mound that resembled a late Classic period pyramid once existed at Louisiana's Troyville site, dating to around 600. The terraced clay pyramid (80 feet high, 180 feet on a side) looked like something borrowed from El Tajín in Veracruz. Kehoe also lists as evidence of Mesoamerican influence Mississippian headdresses, a particularly large chipped-stone knife-blade style, and certain words of possible Mayan derivation in North America, such as the name Powhatan.[6]

She also agrees with Robert Hall's belief that a number of cultural practices or linguistic terms of various eastern North American peoples were ultimately derived from Mesoamerica or shared between Mesoamericans and their more northerly American counterparts. Hall, Kehoe, and others point to such tantalizing parallels because there are few Mesoamerican artifacts north of Mexico. In the Southwest, the remains of macaws, copper bells, chocolate, and the existence of Mesoamerican architectural and iconographic features are the most prominent examples. However, there is only one clear-cut Mesoamerican artifact from a pre-Columbian context in eastern North America: a single, tiny chip of Mexican obsidian at the Spiro site in Oklahoma weighing only a little more than an ounce.[7]

This piece is scant evidence, and it might even have found its way into Oklahoma from Mexico by way of the Rio Grande pueblos, perhaps carried in a pouch with other trinkets across the Santa Fe Trail. However, such indisputable links to Mesoamerica are not what Robert Hall has focused on. Rather, he points to a number of tantalizing cultural parallels, or possible Mesoamerican practices, among peoples from the Great Plains to the eastern seaboard, including the importance of certain numbers (two, four, seven, twelve, and maybe fifty-two and a preoccupation with the Morning and Evening star guises of Venus. Hall also notes the distinctive sacrificial rites of the Pawnee, which parallel the Toltec and Aztec rituals surrounding the flayed god Xipe Totec. These rituals connect human sacrifice and the Mesoamerican New Fire ceremonies to the early Mississippian Green Corn ceremonies, in which pyramid-summit temples and the Corn Mother figured prominently, and to Pawnee and other Plains Indian arrow sacrifices.[8] Other parallels are the Cherokee name for the Corn Mother god, Selu; the common pan–North American associations of the night sky with the underworld and of certain constellations with dogs, gods, trees, and human hands; and an anomalous association among the Osage of "north" with the sky or "up," a Mesoamerican notion.

The early Mississippian period might have been the time when such notions, embedded perhaps within stories (associated with corn agriculture, creation, and rebirth), were introduced into or elaborated upon within the Mississippi valley. It may be no mere coincidence, Hall points out, that Xipe representations in Mexico include vertical painted lines on the face, similar to certain historical-era Plains ritual face painting (including the Honga impersonator mentioned earlier), and perhaps like the striped faces in depictions of the Thunderers or the Morning Star deity—He-who-wears-human-heads-as-earrings or one of the twin Children of the Sun—at the Gottschall Rockshelter or Painted Cave. Indeed, the story of the masculine twins, along with their godlike parents, is remarkably similar to that retold in the Mayan saga recorded in the *Popul Vuh*.

For many archaeologists, the stories intersect in too many ways not to be historically related. In Hall's words, "What the twin stories may relate to more directly is the origin of death and mourning—either of the mother or one twin or both the mother and a twin. . . . The death of the Maya twin Hun Hunahpu relates to mourning, as does the death of the related Winnebago Red Horn more implicitly." Regarding the possible Mesoamerican connections with another Siouan group, Hall compares the Hidatsa story of the twin heroes battling Long Arm, a nighttime "sky chief" of the netherworld, with the Mayan hero twins' encounter with 7 Macaw, lord of the underworld. Characters had heads like rattles in both accounts, and the heroes in both tales managed to impregnate virgins without having intercourse. Moreover, in both Mesoamerican and some North American versions, "the second-born twin, representing the personified placenta or umbilical cord, sometimes has a flint association."[9]

Sometimes in Mesoamerica, the second-born hero twin is depicted as a flint or chipped-stone knife. In Post-Classic central Mexico, this human knife is shown as having anthropomorphic characteristics, including eyes and teeth. According to art historians Mary Miller and Karle Taube, "Chac and Tlaloc, respectively the Maya and Central Mexican hurlers of thunderbolts, were thus the creators of these valued materials." The Mayan god, they add, "usually carries a personified flint in his hand, but sometimes he is himself a personified flint. Among the Aztecs, flint blades [daggers] are also personified, frequently with an open, gnawing mouth, indicating their ability to tear flesh."[10]

As Alice Kehoe has pointed out, another type of chipped-stone dagger, virtually identical in shape and size, made a historically unprecedented appearance in the American midcontinent sometime near the middle of the eleventh century. At the time, these were manufactured near chert (or flint) outcrops in only two places: in the wooded hills of Union County, Illinois, ninety miles south of Cahokia, and in the Ozarks, just twenty miles southeast of Cahokia. Cahokians were the primary consumers of the unusual daggers from both places. Indeed, given the correspondence with Cahokia's sudden burst of constructive energy around 1050, it is possible that Cahokians instigated dagger production in both places, which is why archaeologists have named these objects Ramey knives, after the farm family who had preserved much of the Cahokia site up to 1925.

Ramey knives, it seems, were mass-produced—alongside chipped-stone hoe blades, ceremonial axe heads, maces, and woodworking adze blades—at several villages near the chert quarries. Lithic analysts—those who routinely study ancient stone-tool technologies—have called the production of these objects an industry, one probably only possible with the patronage of Cahokia and other, later Mississippian centers. And while other technologies have local antecedents, the Ramey knives do not. There was nothing like them before about 1050. So the correspondence between the Mesoamerican knife and the Ramey dagger is difficult to ignore, especially when one considers another anomalous artifact that made its appearance shortly after 1050 in the greater Cahokia region: the small, shield-shaped ear ornaments, variously called maskettes or earrings, that seem to fit the description of the objects worn by He-who-wears-human-heads-as-earrings or Red Horn.

The first pair of these earpieces came to the attention of archaeologists and antiquarians after St. Louisans removed the Big

Mound in 1869. Anglo workers had driven their horse-drawn slips to the top and dragged down the huge earthen edifice over a period of weeks. Daguerreotypes made at the time show the sad, slow demise of the mound, the shovel-gouged profiles of the once-prominent tumulus exposing at least one ancient buried summit on which the indigenous people had interred many of their dead. Worn on the ears of the larger of two human skeletons found together in one exposed crypt were delicately crafted maskettes made from copper.[11]

Like others that would turn up years later, the shield-shaped faces on the maskettes were nearly 3 inches high and 1.5 inches wide, with a U-shaped chin and a flattened cranial vault or hat featuring a distinctive stepped outline and a cleft or notch in the forehead. The mouth was no more than a short horizontal line, but the eyes were wide circles centered on an inner pinpoint pupil, giving the face a goggle-eyed appearance. The eyes were unusual (and contrast with the usual lenticular and naturalistic eyes of most early Mississippian art), but the nose was even more so.

When they were first described, before they were connected to the Iowa and Ho-Chunk legends, these and similar maskettes were identified as Long-Nosed God ear ornaments. In fact, the most distinctive thing about all these earpieces discovered across the eastern United States, no matter what they are made from, is the noses. Extraordinarily long and bent or distorted in some fashion, the noses were cleverly welded onto the shield-shaped face of the Big Mound specimens by the aboriginal coppersmith and would have stuck out a full six inches.

An old photograph taken in 1869 of one of the two objects shows that the nose was broken off, perhaps accidentally by the Anglo diggers who found them. After being photographed, the maskettes were promptly misplaced and eventually lost.[12] Archaeologist Stephen Williams located the photograph at Harvard's Peabody Museum years later and, along with his colleague John

Goggin, in 1956 compiled a list of similar objects. Their list would be lengthened by others over the years, and today about twenty Long-Nosed God earpiece finds—isolated objects or pairs of maskettes—are known from the eastern Woodlands and the Plains.[13] Several pairs of these unusual objects were found near Cahokia, the apparent center point of their midcontinental distribution and the likely source of their manufacture.

Wherever found, the maskettes look remarkably alike, having been carved out of large pieces of pearly-white conch shells from the Gulf of Mexico or hammered out of sheet copper from Lake Superior. One isolated find south of Cahokia was made from bone, possibly human. Like Cahokia-style chunkey stones or the carved-flintclay smoking pipes, the rare occurrence yet widespread distribution of these objects suggests to archaeologists that Long-Nosed God maskettes were badges or gifts handed out to people who would have forever after been affiliated with Cahokia.[14]

Several maskette pairs have been found on the ears of male remains at early Mississippian or Cahokia-contact sites around the Midwest and South. Besides those found in the Big Mound, they include a couple of copper heads at the Aztalan site, a well-known palisaded frontier outpost in southern Wisconsin. Gregory Perino excavated a shell pair worn by a man in a blufftop burial south of Cahokia. Farther to the south, a set of copper Long-Nosed God earpieces and a carved Cahokia-style red flintclay pipe were found with a central male burial at the early Caddoan site of Gahagan, in Louisiana.

Another pair of copper ear ornaments was found with the skeleton of an indigenous Illinoisan by a grave robber in the 1960s. They were exceptional specimens and clearly showed that there was more to the noses than anyone had realized: Each was kinked or bent this way and that, giving the final nose a zigzag or accordionlike appearance.

Archaeologist Carol Diaz-Granados and her husband, Jim

Duncan, hypothesized that the bent noses were no accident but precisely what had been intended. They pointed to the painting of He-who-wears-human-heads-as-earrings in the Picture Cave, whose Long-Nosed God earpieces are shown bent upward. They also pointed to two iconographic depictions from the Spiro site, in which men or demigods were illustrated wearing human-head earrings with long noses. And in both cases, the noses are shown zigging and zagging, accordion style.

To explain this, the couple drew an analogy to the Plains Indians adoption ceremonies, in which a war captive or a friendly ally ritually assumed the identity of a dead relative. Such adoptions often involved cutting, or shortening, the nose of the adopted brother. For some war captives, nose cutting marked their new status. Duncan and Diaz-Granados believed that the bending of the Long-Nosed God maskette noses symbolized the same sort of thing. The missing noses on the Big Mound earpieces, they argued, also might have been an act by the ancient Indian elite to show that the man who wore them was totally "civilized."

Robert Hall suggests that the idea of a goggle-eyed god as represented by the earrings might have been around for centuries, although not as ornaments worn on the ears. He sees hints of round eyes and bifurcated abstract figures in the Hopewellian art of the Middle Woodland period. Duncan and Diaz-Granados point to a painting of an underwater deity or mythical snake god also with goggle eyes, in Missouri's Painted Cave. Archaeologist Brad Koldehoff points to the dot-in-circle eyes of pre-Mississippian animal carvings, which might anticipate the water-spirit imagery that reappears in the Long-Nosed God maskettes. If these archaeologists are correct, the association of the circular-eye motif with an underworld god or water-spirit might help explain the goggle eyes of the maskettes.

Of course, various Mexican earth, rain, and water gods were

also known by their goggle-shaped eyes. The ever-changing pantheon of Mesoamerican gods included an earth/rain/fertility god variously named Tlaloc or Chac. Both, at least in their typical guises, had goggle eyes, long or twisted noses, and fangs. These attributes recall, in a sort of mix-and-match fashion, the stories mentioned earlier of various American Indian hero twins, particularly Wild or Lost Boy, Afterbirth Boy, Thrown-Away, and the Foolish One.

In an alternative interpretation, Hall has suggested that Xolotl, a twin of the Mexican god Quetzalcoatl, might be the Long-Nosed God.[15] But he conceded that it might also be Tlaloc or Chac, as James Griffin once thought, or possibly some composite of all of these. In any case, it seems unlikely, especially in light of the fact that ancient Mesoamericans were themselves always reinterpreting the gods, that North Americans would have fully understood or perfectly transferred to the Mississippi valley some set of meanings or mythical associations of any particular Mesoamerican god.

However, that the Long-Nosed Gods of early Cahokia and its outliers were originally Mexican seems a compelling idea, because of the multiple corresponding traits of Cahokian and Mexican imagery: goggle eyes, distorted noses, and (via historical accounts) hints of fangs. The goggle eyes may be rooted in pre-Mississippian traditions of midwestern peoples, while the long noses have no clear antecedents in North America. In addition, the Cahokia-Mexican connection seems compelling because of timing: The appearance of both the human-head earrings and the daggers follows on the heels of Cahokia's big bang, which, in turn, corresponds with Mesoamerica's expansive Post-Classic Toltec period, dated to the early eleventh century and once thought to have involved an empire linked to the Mexican city of Tula. Most archaeologists agree that, at the very least, the Toltec expansion involved the spread of militaristic and religious ideals across language and political boundaries in Mesoamerica. Perhaps, thinks Alice Kehoe, such Post-Classic sensibilities might have infiltrated the Mississippi valley as well at this same time.

Last, the Cahokia-Mexican connection seems possible because both the Mississippian Long-Nosed Gods and the Ramey daggers have actual Mesoamerican counterparts, in either material or oral-narrative form, linking them to mythical accounts of twin heroes and the forces of creation. Even the practice of wearing human-head earpieces may be Mesoamerican. In central Mexico or the Mayan region, different gods were identifiable by their distinctive ear ornaments and related headgear. So when the Ho-Chunk hero He-who-wears-human-heads-as-earrings declared himself an immortal in front of his brothers, he may have been revealing himself to be a Mesoamerican god.[16] Such borrowing by Cahokians and others should be expected. Mesoamerica wasn't that far away, and besides, the big bang of native North America, centered on the events at Cahokia, involved groups of people reimagining their place in human creation by drawing various legends and stories together into a coherent narrative. What more powerful way to solidify one's narrative claim to creation—and all the economic and political benefits thereof—than by linking oneself to the great cities of central Mexico and the Yucatán? It is likely that the legends and rumors of such places circulated in the local lore of many North Americans, most (or all) of whom would have never had the opportunity to visit Mesoamerica.

There are many accounts and lines of hard evidence, argues ethnohistorian Mary Helms, that emergent rulers attempted to control others by controlling esoteric knowledge.[17] A person whose mind encompasses esoterica is inherently more powerful than others. Hence, ritual specialists and leaders actively sought to understand the obscure by traveling to remote locations to commune with supernatural forces (via vision quests, for example) and to learn from foreigners. If a would-be Cahokian ruler or ruling group had not yet traveled far afield before the supernova of 1054, it is likely that they did shortly thereafter, possibly to Mesoamerica.

While they were there, the Cahokians would have seen or learned great and mysterious things; upon their return, their stories and newfound powers might have attracted many followers. Returning leaders, if astute, would have then connected, through symbols and stories, the strange new knowledge acquired in the far-off land to sensibilities, traditions, or beliefs at home. The local people might have been willing to tolerate much in the way of strange new ideas if built on homegrown principles. For instance, a Long-Nosed God might have been novel, but a goggle-eyed god, long-nosed or not, might have tapped local sensibilities. Likewise, worshipping gods that had a human form might have been foreign to many midwestern people in 1050, but if those godlike people assumed the qualities of traditional sky and earth spirits, people might have been willing to make sacrifices in order to accommodate them.

In such ways, the cult of a Corn Mother or of twin Thunderers, even if referencing far-off Mexican gods, might have nonetheless become an undeniably homegrown Cahokian phenomenon. In fairly short order, perhaps aided by the supernova, New Cahokia would have become a political and religious dynamo that assumed a life all its own. Others seeking esoteric knowledge and legitimacy in the remote corners of the Midwest, Plains, and South might have traveled to Cahokia to learn what they could.

Even today, certain places—Paris, New York, Hollywood—or peoples are recognized by others as more culturally sophisticated or knowledgeable. In Indian country, the Wichita looked to the Pawnee for cultural inspiration, and the Crow admired and emulated the Mandan, whom they viewed as cosmopolitan. How many more groups would have looked to New Cahokia in its day? In such a way, perhaps, Cahokia really was a Post-Classic city, a stand-in for Mesoamerica with a historical impact on the rest of North America as great as that of any Mesoamerican city on its own people.

11

TREASURE MAPS OF THE PAST

AT THE EDGE OF THE MIGHTY Mississippi River, Terry Norris, chief archaeologist of the U.S. Army Corps of Engineers, based in St. Louis, Missouri, was examining some rock debris he had found. At this very spot—Thebes Gap, a short and narrow, flood-plainless bottleneck in the river 130 miles south of Cahokia, near the Mississippi's confluence with the Ohio—late-eighteenth-century French cartographer Nicolas de Finiels had mapped a *chaîne de rochers,* or "chain of rocks," that jutted well out into the river, a landmark well known to later boatmen, engineers, cartographers, and explorers. The location was also known for a high bank of pure white clay overlaying dark red clay, all visible from the river. Native Americans had probably extracted the clay to use for paints and high-quality pots. Nineteenth-century Euroamericans mined it for the same purpose.

Given the treacherous rocks, Thebes Gap was a natural stopping point for weary travelers, a good place from which to portage one's goods, perhaps after staying the night. An enterprising

Spanish colonist, in fact, built a trading post just south of the rocks in the 1700s. Lewis and Clark, who stopped here in November 1803, described the spot as

> pretty well covered with large rock of many tons weight lying in a loose manner on the serface [sic] or but partially bedded in the earth. . . . [T]he land is of an inferior quality on these hills being a stiff white clay soil.—observed a very fine quarry of white freestone on the eastern bank of a small run which made into the river.[1]

In his official duties as corps archaeologist, Norris had been checking on one of the boulders the size of small trucks that remained: a twelve-ton petroglyph-covered rock usually submerged in the water. He needed to be sure that the engineers' riprap and check-dams, intended to keep the channel open, would not damage this important natural and cultural landmark. The Mississippi was unusually low after a winter of near-drought conditions out in the Missouri River basin, and the entire rock sat on the bank exposed.

These conditions had allowed Norris to see something no archaeologist had noticed before: There were large chunks, or "flakes," of the rock lying about, most showing the telltale signs of having been "knapped"—chipped and shaped by ancient people. When these chunks were compared to ancient artifacts, Norris realized that the knapped rock material was a red-stained quartzite identical to the raw material used to make Cahokia-style chunkey stones. He had discovered the likely source of the previously unsourced raw material used in the production of these all-important artifacts.

Norris jokes about his curious ability to make singular archaeological discoveries. It began in his teenage years, when he was on hand as a crew member of Melvin Fowler's Mound 72 dig and accidentally turned up some of the famous buried arrowheads. In the late 1970s, he found a lost French colonial fort by looking through aerial photographs. In the early 1980s, in a farmer's field, he located the original site of the French town of Ste. Genevieve, which historians had assumed had been washed away by the Mississippi River. At about the same time, he stumbled onto a river-scoured Mississippian site where the remains of ancient houses and household artifacts sat exposed on the surface in a most unusual manner. Then, in 1982, Norris found one of the rarest of Mississippian objects, an elongated ceremonial axe head—sometimes called a spud—while looking for French colonial house sites in the original village of Cahokia (distinct from and several miles south of the ancient city).

On a sunny September morning in 2005, Norris returned to the boulder-strewn site on the banks of the Mississippi. He had made the chunkey-stone connection, but the significance of the rock-art panel had not yet sunk in. Norris wondered whether the petroglyphs on the boulder somehow marked the spot as the chunkey-stone source. He also wondered about an earlier identification of a large squiggly line on the rock as a serpent. Archaeologists have long interpreted such lines as representations of snakes or snakelike supernatural beings that American Indians believed dwelled under the earth or in deep water, but this one was not simply a coiled snake or a squiggly line with two end points. Instead, this line cut across the entire rock, bending from top to bottom. On either side were peck marks in clusters, some closer than others and spaced as if to indicate specific places east and west of the line. Some of the marks were near or connected by secondary pecked lines that radiated to other portions of the rock panel.

Norris thought that the serpentine lines looked more like the representation of a river that began in the north and curved southeastward. Straining to see the individual pecked motifs, he grabbed an old Styrofoam cup that had floated down the river, just a couple of steps away. He filled it with river water, which he then splashed onto the rock. Immediately, in the morning sunshine, the rock art popped out clearly from the surface.

A meandering line, a large eye, a moccasin print, an eagle or falcon glyph, and a host of other unusual lines and clustered marks had been hammered into the rock. The pecked marks are rare, and almost unheard of in association with an elongated meandering line, which itself was unusual. This was not an average set of petroglyphs. But then, this was not an ordinary natural or cultural site. It was a stopping point, a constriction in the river that required careful navigation by travelers. Few canoeing along at any point in human history could have missed the white and red clay bank and the multi-ton boulders around which the Mississippi River waters rushed. Looking down at the wet array of pecked lines and glyphs, Norris realized that this rock-art panel was a map.

The historical significance of Norris's rock-art map, one of only a few such cartographic representations known from pre-Columbian North America, lies in its location and in how the lines and glyphs are arranged. The bird of prey glyph, probably a falcon, is shown folding or flapping its wings after landing, a pose that suggests it might be a place glyph—a symbol that marks a spot or identifies a people living in some place. The pecked markings may be trails and town site locations.

Several years ago, Patricia O'Brien, a veteran Cahokia archaeologist who worked with Bareis, Porter, and the other original salvage archaeologists in the 1960s, suggested that similar rock art found a little closer to Cahokia marked the political boundaries of the Cahokian nation, or what she called the "Ramey state" (again, after the farm family, the Rameys, whose land was sold to the state of Illinois to create the Cahokia Mounds State Historic Site). Her reasons have struck some fellow archaeologists as compelling. For one, native people often ventured into the no-man's-lands between nations for vision quests that involved creating or viewing rock art. For another, Indians were known to use place glyphs like signposts to communicate with passersby. Indeed, some southern warriors posted such signs at the edges of the towns or territories that they planned to attack as a way of declaring war. Although not quite the same thing, Norris's rock-art site was a natural anomaly and stopping point; it might have been a good place to warn travelers of the people-of-the-falcon who lived beyond the rock to the north.

Not all archaeologists feel comfortable with such speculative suggestions. Many remain skeptical of the idea that a rock-art panel could double as a cartographic depiction. Some resist because it isn't completely accepted that pre-Columbian indigenous people had the wherewithal to make maps. Others might be skeptical because map reading is not an exact science, and any cartographic representation can be interpreted in multiple ways. Still others prefer to interpret the motifs on the rock-art panel individually, believing each glyph to have a deep religious meaning, rather than interpreting the set as a storyboard or a map that located people and their narratives in real time. By this line of thinking, Thebes Gap was a remote, mysterious location in the ancient past, and people went there for vision quests to commune with supernatural forces. These ancient people may have pecked the symbols we see today into the rock as a part of such a ritual experience.

Such alternatives are not necessarily inconsistent with seeing the Thebes Gap rock-art panel as a map. And if it was, the implication is that the people who traveled along the river, through a world that Cahokia helped to shape, had a clear sense of territoriality and political identity, if not a distinct cultural heritage. A map might be necessary to navigate or remember boundaries, and boundaries in turn suggest a degree of social complexity born of a complex political history.

Of course, maps were made by many indigenous American peoples in centuries past, the most famous being early-eighteenth-century hide maps that the Chickasaw and Choctaw used to orient themselves in a politically partitioned South. A map drawn on hide was handed to Champlain in 1605 to help him navigate through the Northeast. Other maps were sketched on birch bark or engraved in wood by indigenous traders, travelers, artists, or warriors. Certain Ojibwa, Hidatsa, and Ho-Chunk maps from the nineteenth century look a little like the diagram pecked into Norris's large river rock. In fact, there are more than a dozen other known rock-art maps, from Arizona, California, Colorado, Idaho, and North Carolina, not counting those images that seem to map the night sky or a particular supernova in 1054.[2]

This isn't too surprising. So common was indigenous map-making or picture-writing to native North America that a government document hundreds of pages thick was dedicated to it in 1893.[3] A map is not a complicated abstraction, after all, but one kind of narrative account—a storyboard or spatial text that locates features, places, pathways, characters, ideas, or events in space or time. A site at Chaco Canyon showing the supernova is, in essence, a map of the cosmos in 1054 that locates the event within the Chacoan landscape. So, too, are representations of the supernova in Missouri and picture stories of battles drawn by American Indians on hides, on teepees, and, later, in ledger books. What distinguishes these various inscriptions is how, or to what degree, features, places, characters, ideas, and events were spatialized and temporalized, which is to say depicted with reference to locations or the passage of time.

Like other preindustrial peoples around the world, most pre-Columbian North Americans did not conceive or quantify time and space the way historians and cartographers do today. Anthropologists and archaeologists have described this in different ways, often counterposing a daily, experiential time to a kind of genealogical or historical time and, beyond that, a mythical, monumental, or, one might say, ritual time.[4] These were never rigidly distinguished, any more than natural forces were distinguished from supernatural ones. This being the case, ancient maps may not always take an expected form. Not every old map might fit Western cartographic conventions, with a huge X marking the spot where archaeologists will find the answers to their questions. Much rock art was thoroughly embedded within the spatial and temporal fields wherein people, places, and nonhuman forces were thought to coincide, meaning that certain Native American maps may not even be found in one place but spread across the landscape like clues in a treasure hunt. Among various Plains people, the "very earth and sky" could be read like maps.[5]

Recent efforts by archaeologists and art historians to decipher the symbolism of the Mississippians, including their rock art, tend to downplay this idea. Instead, they focus on a kind of glyph-specific interpretive approach that assumes Native American artwork does not show actual people in historical scenes; rather, the actions depicted almost always occurred in mythical time and in supernatural realms and thus do not represent reality.[6] And while there is much in their arguments with which to agree, there is a potential problem with the degree to which some overgeneralize the meanings of specific symbols.

In characterizing Native American art as depictions of supernatural scenes and otherworldly action of timeless meaning to all Mississippians, archaeologists risk denying indigenous people a certain sort of history—one that locates actual people and events in this world (or between worlds), much like Terry Norris's Thebes Gap map. Such action need not be dissociated from superhuman and mythical associations for the maps or storyboards to portray a real world of moving and thinking human beings. Indeed, genealogical time is commonly a mix of both. The results are legends and oral histories—stories that many believe to have been true, if embellished.

At a conference in 1999, Carrie Wilson, a member of the Quapaw Nation of Oklahoma and an advocate of their cultural history, engaged a small group of archaeologists in a casual conversation about this issue. She had been showing around a photograph of a famous Quapaw bison robe painted during the seventeenth century and was interested in their gut reactions to her provocative idea that it depicted a story rooted in historical events. The robe had a pentagonal outline delimiting a design field showing people moving—dancing or migrating—along its perimeter. At the center were large images of the sun and the moon.

Could it be, she asked, that this robe might tell the story of the ancestral Quapaw emigrating out of Cahokia some four centuries earlier? Wilson proposed that the drawing depicted the layout of downtown Cahokia, the pentagonal shape of the robe's border conforming to the site's massive palisade wall, and the sun representing the great pyramid, Monks Mound. She had heard accounts about the Quapaw being the "downriver" people who had left their Dhegihan homeland first, and who might later be known by other names (Osage, Ponca, Kansa, and Omaha). Perhaps, she thought, these stories were the traces of the oral-historical links long sought by those interested in indigenous heritage.

Wilson's argument was consistent with a point that preeminent Maya archaeologist David Friedel, of Southern Methodist University in Dallas, had made earlier that evening in a plenary talk entitled "Killing the Gods and Burning the Thrones." He had suggested that Cahokia—this early Mississippian behemoth of a site—was a founding city like those known in other parts of the world. Such cities had tremendous historical effects on the peoples who came later. They were the subject of legends and visits by pilgrims for centuries thereafter. In Mexico, for instance, certain researchers believe that the early Classic-period Mexican city of Teotihuacán had profound impacts on the Maya to the east in the Yucatán, Belize, and Guatemala. Indeed, the great sites of Tikal and Copán had probably been ruled at some point by elites from, or connected to, Teotihuacán. The first ruler of Copán, named Yax-Kuk-Mo, seems to have impersonated one of the Teotihuacáno gods—the goggle-eyed rain god known to later Nahuatl-speakers as Tlaloc. Like the art of ancient Greece or Egypt, the Mayan glyph-writing told stories of rulers who did great things and, occasionally, commingled with gods.

The odd thing about Cahokia is that, Carrie Wilson's ideas notwithstanding, the epic stories of a founding city seem to be missing in the eastern Woodlands. It should have been commemorated in tales and songs, as was the case with Chaco Canyon in the Southwest, where archaeologist Steve Lekson has asserted that the legendary place of modern Puebloan peoples, White Town, may be a reference to the Great Houses of that place among the later native people.[7] By contrast, in the eastern United States, there are no oral-history references to Cahokia, only vague origin stories of people who originated in the east, near big rivers. Among the Pawnee, Robert Hall once found reference to a Red City that he thought might have been Cahokia, but it turned out to be a later reference to St. Louis.

In earlier attempts to use historical accounts to explain the origins of various Plains and southern peoples, the strange absence of references to Cahokia was not given much thought. More recently, though, archaeologists have begun to open up the discussion by casting their interpretive nets a bit more widely, using maps and stories to guide their research, in the spirit of Wilson's provocative thinking. And in attempting to explain the absence of Cahokia in indigenous narratives, archaeologists wonder whether the living conditions in and around the city were not so great. Perhaps the Cahokians pushed the envelope of authority, taxation, and oppression too far.

Maybe, by the twelfth century, people were seeking to escape Cahokia, and their desire to forget it—and create a more perfect, communal post-Cahokian society—were all a part of starting over. Whatever the specifics, the curious nature of Cahokia's almost nonexistent cultural memory remains a piece of the puzzle for which archaeologists like Terry Norris will continue to dig.

12

HIGH PLAINS DRIFTING

ON A HIGH, windswept hilltop in Wyoming sits the Big Horn Medicine Wheel. A ninety-foot-diameter arrangement of small boulders positioned in the shape of a mandala or pinwheel, it is one of more than a hundred such sacred shrines found far out on the Plains. Its circular perimeter is intersected by many lines of rocks radiating out from its center, presumably referencing celestial alignments—the risings and settings of the sun, moon, and stars at key points in the year. In this way, according to Robert Hall, World Center Shrines like this were astronomical observatories.

But, as with many of these ancient observatories, including Cahokia's Woodhenge, the Big Horn Medicine Wheel's alignments aren't perfect, and the real importance of the monument is its overall symbolism. The circle of stones, it is said, represents the earth. The radiating lines, giving the shrine the appearance of a starburst, were the sacred paths into the center of the world. Believers still make pilgrimages to this site, following any number of personal paths to this center point, leaving offerings to ensure balance and harmony in their lives.

Among many Plains peoples, from Dhegiha-Siouan and Cad-doan speakers in the south to the Crow in the north, the living would mourn the dead and "renew the world" during rites held at such shrines. One rite practiced by several groups, the Sun Dance, took place in modest wooden-pole "corrals" that looked like small versions of Cahokia's Woodhenge. Inside, mourners would call upon the creator gods to assist the community, sometimes also wish-ing vengeance upon their enemies. Then a man impersonating the good twin—Civilized Boy, Spring Boy, Lodge Boy, and so forth—would step forward. Having fasted for days, he would have his pec-toral flesh skewered and tethered to the central post. Tension was applied, pulling at the soft tissue until the skewers were ripped out.

This bizarre ritual might well have begun at Cahokia as part of a cult practice associated with the Woodhenge, then been adopted by others, just as chunkey, Cahokia-style smoking pipes, and Mississippian temple-ritual practices generally were adopted by people along the Mississippi River and into the Plains and the South. It is likely that such rituals and dances as performed inside Cahokia's Woodhenge, for instance, were spectacles, like so much that Cahokia had to offer, accompanied by the prayers, chants, and drummings of hundreds if not thousands of onlooking farmers, priests, and pilgrims.

Today the reconstructed Woodhenge sits at the western edge of the Cahokia Mounds State Historic Site, mute save for the sounds of traffic on the county highway to its south and the interstate high-way to its north. The treasures that excavations have revealed are a tribute not only to the greatness of the city itself but also to the many archaeologists who worked tirelessly to widen the scope of what is known and understood about Cahokia and its inhabitants.

Up until his death, Warren Wittry met a few local enthusiasts before each winter-solstice dawn in the middle of the Woodhenge reconstruction. From there, they watched the sun rise from behind Monks Mound and the red cedar post that marked the solstice sunrise position, about 30 degrees south of east. In the months that followed, the rising sun tracked a little farther north each day, a harbinger of the eventual return of springtime's plant and animal life.

Warren Wittry and Robert Hall grew up together as boys, continued together as high school and college classmates, joined the navy together, and began their professional careers together by working in the Great Plains. Later, they dug at Cahokia's Tract 15A in successive field seasons. They were, as much as any friends can be, brothers in practice and in spirit. And both together and separately, they transformed archaeologists' understanding of ancient Cahokia. When Wittry died, Hall performed a private ceremony at the reconstruction of the Woodhenge, which Wittry had discovered in 1961.

Balance eventually returned to Preston Holder and Joyce Wike's world as well. After leaving his Cahokia research behind, Holder went back to work on his primary love and the subject of his doctoral work: Plains village archaeology. In 1958, he accepted the chair of the Department of Anthropology at Nebraska, where he and Joyce and their colleagues trained the next generation of Plains archaeologists. Holder's own dissertation had focused on the protohistoric Arikara, a Caddoan agricultural group that had moved up into the Missouri River region during or after the heyday of Cahokia. He speculated on the historical relationships between the various peoples who had migrated onto the Plains and their Mississippian antecedents at places such as Cahokia and Spiro.[1] To the end, Holder believed that the histories of the Plains and Cahokia were closely linked. But in 1980, not having completed manuscripts in which he might report and interpret his most cherished Junkyard and Kunnemann mound digs at Cahokia, the aged and now terminally ill bohemian eccentric dictated his last few recollections to his wife on his deathbed.

As a later Cahokia archaeologist and FAI-270 veteran would discover, the historical connections between Cahokia and the Plains that had so concerned Wittry, Hall, Holder, and the rest were in no way simple or straightforward. They would require future generations to pick up the mantle and dedicate their lives to digging for the whole truth. Certainly, the pre-Columbian farmers possibly related to or descended from Cahokians had not gradually "evolved" to life on the Plains, as the typical conservative archaeological storyline went. The end of Cahokia might have been terribly unpleasant to experience; the cultural landscape it helped shape in the Plains turned ugly in the years after Cahokia dissolved, as exemplified by endemic violence against men, women, and children in the Illinois River valley to the north and, more forcefully, by the events revealed in one specific horrific discovery at Crow Creek, South Dakota.

Before moving on to work for Chuck Bareis and Jim Porter on the FAI-270 highway project, Thomas Emerson had worked for the state of South Dakota. In 1978, in his role as a state staff archaeologist, he was asked to inspect a well-known village site along Crow Creek where looters were digging human bones out of the banks near the stream's confluence with the Missouri River. He arrived to find the locals indiscriminately digging into a massive deposit of human bones. Putting an end to the looting, he began excavations that would last most of that year. During that time he and his crew received death threats from a faction of Lakota men who were understandably upset, at first with the looting and then with the professional excavation of the human remains. In their disgust, they were initially unwilling to believe that American Indians, possibly even their ancestors, had committed an atrocity such as seemed apparent in what Emerson had uncovered.

Emerson and his crew had found a Native American massacre, probably a near extermination of an entire proto-Arikara village. It appears that at some time during the fourteenth century, eight hundred or so villagers living in the fifty large lodges of this agricultural settlement had been attacked by a longtime enemy, quite possibly a large group of Siouan-speaking warriors. While the proto-Arikara Crow Creek villagers were working on a new fortification ditch and palisade wall, the enemy descended with overwhelming killing power. The assailants may have taken some of the village women captive, setting the lodges ablaze as they went, some with people still inside. The rest of the men, women, and children they clubbed to death. The war party scalped many and then mutilated the bodies as one might butcher bison, dismembering them, bashing in teeth, and cutting out tongues in an excess of murderous zeal.[2]

The Crow Creek massacre was unlike anything ever experienced during Cahokia's heyday three centuries earlier, but there is still reason to tie its causes to a long chain of events and disputes over social boundaries that stretch deep into the past, back to Cahokia and perhaps, indirectly, to the large-scale violence of its ridgetop-mound sacrifices, among other things. The ethnic landscape along the Mississippi, and probably into the Plains, had been made complex over the course of the Mississippian period, as Norris's rock-art map attests.

In addition, Cahokians, Emerson now suspects, had transformed the rules of military engagement as they established their cultural preeminence over the many other, less-organized midwestern peoples of the time. Before Cahokia, tensions between kin groups or villages would occasionally boil over into small-scale conflicts or blood feuds, a few people might have lost their scalps and their lives in the occasional skirmish or ambuscade, but organized military action was essentially unknown up to 1050.

Even during Cahokia's heyday, certain groups might have avoided fighting by playing chunkey, winner take all. Distant visitors or teams might have arrived to compete in this aggressive face-off between foes. Clearly, some visitors left with the chunkey stones, among other things, as evidenced by the distinctively shaped Cahokia-style stones (first identified by Gregory Perino), often made out of the Thebes Gap quartzite quarried at Terry Norris's rock-art site. Perhaps Cahokians had even sent envoys or missionaries, chunkey rollers in one hand and war clubs in the other, out into the hinterlands with the purpose of making peace or political alliances, as conceived by Guy Gibbon and Robert Hall.[3] Late-nineteenth-century anthropologist Alice Fletcher recounted a historical-period instance of such a long-distance peace party trekking across the Great Plains. They carried the peace pipe, called the Hako or Calumet, before them.

> The Hako party was an impressive sight as it journeyed over the country. It could never be mistaken for an ordinary group of hunters, warriors, or travelers. At the head of the long procession, sufficiently in advance to be distinguished from the others, walked three men—the Ku'rahus, holding before him the brown-eagle feathered stem, on his right the chief, grasping with both hands the wildcat skin and Mother Corn, and at his left the assistant Ku'rahus, bearing the white-eagle feathered stem. . . . Behind them walked the doctors with their insignia, the white eagle wings; then the singers with the drum, and behind them the men and women of the party with the ponies with gifts and needed supplies of food. . . . Over the wide prairie for miles and miles this order was preserved day after day until the journey came to an end. If from some distant vantage point a war party should descry the procession, the leader would silently turn his men that they might not meet the Hako party, for the feathered stems are mightier than the warrior; before them he must lay down his weapon, forget his anger, and be at peace.[4]

Of course, the possible existence of Cahokian peacemaking envoys would not preclude the existence of equally organized

Cahokian war parties that might have kept the peace through strategic violence. Cahokians could have sent warrior squadrons in canoes to subordinate if not eliminate rivals, troublemakers, and any upstarts who sought to challenge the city's grip on the Mississippi and its tributaries. In this way, they could have established and enforced a central-valley-wide peace of sorts, a veritable Pax Cahokiana.

The killing techniques at Crow Creek probably weren't so unlike those perfected by Cahokians, which involved the use of standardized shock weapons, particularly macelike war clubs and shields, in hand-to-hand combat. The Cahokians had commemorated such tactics in two different red flintclay statues carved in the early twelfth century. One of these, found in a cemetery between Cahokia and Thebes Gap, shows a naked warrior, his long hair tied in a ponytail, crouching behind a large wooden shield. The other was buried a couple of centuries later at Spiro, Oklahoma. It shows a Cahokian in full battle gear, wearing thick cloth armor to protect his head, arms, and legs from enemy blows, with a shield swung around onto his back (though ordinarily it would have been held with his left arm). Apparently, the shield was moved out of the way because the warrior has his hands full. He is shown leaning over a subdued enemy, naked and crouched close to the ground in front of him. In his left fist, the Cahokian warrior holds the long hair of his victim. In his right, he holds the end of a chipped-stone mace, a sort of battle-axe manufactured in southern Illinois, having just slammed its sharp edge into the face of the captive.

This last carving may memorialize the scalping or killing of a particular enemy, perhaps commemorating the actual military victory of a powerful Cahokian over a political rival, or it might celebrate in general what Cahokians did to their enemies. It might even illustrate a mythic event. In any case, this sort of warfare was probably intended to intimidate an enemy if not also to achieve a strategic military goal. What the enemies of Cahokia might have learned from such assaults, however, was how to attack others using formations of warriors wielding clubs. When Cahokia's ability to project military power collapsed, dissolving the Pax Cahokiana and opening up a power vacuum and, later, a vacant quarter in middle America, knowledge of the new tactics remained. These tactics celebrated armored warriors with shock weapons in much the same way as did a new violent game that became increasingly popular over the same time period and, ultimately, supplanted chunkey as the official sport of American Indians in eastern North America. That game was stickball, the "little brother of war."

Without the mantle of Cahokian peace covering the Mississippi, village-based tensions and ethnic-level struggles reemerged, with squadrons of warriors prowling the landscape and with one village's warriors fighting those of other villages. Exacerbating the power vacuum were the effects of the Cahokian diaspora. With the reduction and fragmentation of Cahokian society in the late twelfth and the thirteenth centuries came waves of migrations and a reshuffling of populations, homelands, and ethnic boundaries in the Mississippi and Missouri river basins. In some quarters, social chaos ensued.

Of course, the violence that erupted in those days can only be indirectly credited to Cahokia or its failure to sustain itself. But for whatever reasons, ethnic tensions worsened as peoples moved up and along the Missouri River from the Caddoan south, the Siouan east, and the Algonkian north. By the time of the Euroamerican invasion, discrete Indian nations claimed specific regions of the midcontinent and South. In a very real way, the displaced descendants, allies, and distant cousins of ancient Cahokia truly shaped America's westward expansion. All travelers on the Missouri had to negotiate safe passage with these fierce peoples. For a time, Thomas Jefferson and his agents, including William Clark, were confused about how to navigate the complex cultural landscape of the Louisiana Purchase, the keystone to Jefferson's vision of America. For instance, the Osage—possible descendants of certain Cahokian émigrés—blocked commercial expansion and forced prolonged negotiations. Likewise, the Pawnee—whose ancestors knew or might also have been Cahokians—held key portions of the Missouri and remained loyal allies of Spain into the American period, forcing drawn-out negotiations by United States Indian agents. In the late nineteenth century, many young Pawnee men achieved notoriety as scouts attached to U.S. cavalry units, helping them subdue their old adversaries on the Plains, including their Siouan (Lakota) and Algonkian (Cheyenne) enemies.

Explaining America's history is contingent on understanding its complex indigenous history, and that, in turn, depends on understanding pre-Columbian America's experiment in civilization—a unique blend of church and state, locals and immigrants, male and female narratives, and foreign ideas and local traditions that gave it an expansionist quality archaeologists must strive to understand. Some questions remain mysteries for future archaeologists to solve: Did knowledge of Mesoamerica play a part in Cahokia's creation? How much of a catalyst was the supernova of 1054? Was the cult of the Thunderer twins and Corn Mother goddess established or transformed in Cahokia's theatrical ridgetop mortuaries, with their many human sacrifices? How important was the allegiance and cooperation of common farmers? Were migrations key to the big bang? Did Cahokia's descendants consciously attempt to forget the city?

Some answers will be found in the accounts of early Euroamerican travelers, the legends of native people, the words of dying native tongues, and the dark corners of grottoes. Others will be discovered among the hundreds of houses excavated at immigrant villages, the bodies of sacrificed young women in ridgetop mounds, and the heirloomed rolling stones and Long-Nosed God earpieces carried off to the four winds. No one line of evidence, of course, will lead to a perfect understanding of Mississippian civilization, any more than will any one map, one legend, or one group of descendants.

Many American Indian peoples actively and creatively constructed a universe that radically redefined their history. Such a basic
realization is a major step forward in understanding the story of ancient North America and in mapping out the connections between
past and present. There may be multiple ways of understanding
those connections, but it seems clear that, at one time, they all con-
verged at Cahokia.

The words of the Iowa storyteller, who relayed the account of
Human-head-earrings in the early twentieth century, can be
adapted to make this larger point: The legends of a place, time, and
people will live on. They are stories told with words and through
art, but they are fully narrated through the material remains of that
which all people did in life. Thus, the legends are stories of life and
death, earth and sky, and men and women linking past and present. Corn grows and is harvested, summer turns to winter, people
leave and return, and civilizations rise and fall. Inevitably, night
follows day, as the Evening Star follows the Morning Star. At
night, the sky fills with reminders of the past until the rising sun
dissolves the darkness, balancing all.

ACKNOWLEDGMENTS

A COMPLETE SET OF 1968 World Book encyclopedias, a gift for my three sisters and me that our mother bought from a traveling salesman, opened the door to archaeology. I also inherited her rock collection, arrowheads, and all those family curios, many of which I discovered hidden in drawers, resting on shelves in outbuildings, or stuck away on the upper floor of our mysterious and spider-infested old barn. I saw Cahokia first with my father. In the late 1960s, he would pass through what was then the Cahokia Mounds State Park on the summer Tuesdays of my youth, delivering wholesale goods to businesses such as the Indian Mound Motel on the far side.

Over the years, I have benefited greatly from my teachers, advisors, and friends: Sidney Denny, William Woods, Terry Norris, Brad Koldehoff, Jon Muller, and, especially, Henry Wright, Richard Ford, John O'Shea, Jeff Parsons, and Warren Whatley at the University of Michigan. I also appreciate the help, advice, and tolerance of a couple of generations of the old American Bottom archaeology

mafia: Robert Hall, Elizabeth Benchley, Thomas Emerson, Andrew
Fortier, Pat Munson, Robert Salzer, John Kelly, the late Charles
Bareis, Melvin Fowler, James B. Griffin, Al Meyer, Gregory Perino,
and Warren Wittry. Robert Hall, Thomas Emerson, Alice Kehoe,
Robert Hormell, Andrew Fortier, and Bill Iseminger read earlier
sections of this book and provided me with much-appreciated ad-
vice, commentary, and correction. A special thanks to them and to
Barbara Hall, Steve Lekson, Tim McCleary, Al Meyer, Pat Munson,
Terry Norris, Kirk Perry, Sue Linder-Linsley, Dale Henning, David
Friedel, Tom Riley, Jerome Rose, Joyce Wike, Carrie Wilson, and
John Kelly for their thoughts, discussions, and interviews, some long
ago and brief and some more recent and drawn out.

   Thanks to series editor Colin Calloway, Carolyn Carlson, Ellen
Garrison, and, especially, Kevin Doughten at Viking Penguin, my
years of research around Cahokia have been honed down into the
present book. That research was originally funded by the National
Science Foundation, National Geographic Society, Wenner-Gren
Foundation for Anthropological Research, Cahokia Mounds Mu-
seum Society, U.S. Army Corps of Engineers (St. Louis District),
Illinois Department of Transportation, Illinois Transportation Archaeological Research Program, University of Illinois, University of
Oklahoma, State University of New York, Illinois Historic Preservation Agency, Illinois State Museum, and the Illinois Division of
Natural Resources. Bits and pieces of the research also benefited
from my interactions and time spent at the School for Advanced
Research in Santa Fe, New Mexico, with special thanks to SAR
president James F. Brooks.

   A chunk of this book was drafted in Oaxaca City, Mexico, and
I'm especially grateful to my hosts and friends at the Hotel Casa
Arnel, a haven for archaeologists, blue-staters, and other world
travelers alike. Arnel, Lillian, Luis Marie, Maria, Panto, and Angel:
muchas gracias. To my fellow travelers passing through Oaxaca
from British Columbia, Oregon, the United Kingdom, Spain, and

Australia, including Craig, Erin, and Bruce; Cathy, Marianne, and Lois (the Tres Mujeres); and especially Vivian and Christia, thank you! Last, my heartfelt gratitude goes to Susan, my wife and fellow wayfarer, who has been with me in so many places, real and imagined, past and present.

NOTES

CHAPTER 1: THE MOTHER OF NATIVE NORTH AMERICA

1. First published in 1997 in *Cahokia: Domination and Ideology in the Mississippian World,* edited by T. R. Pauketat and T. E. Emerson, University of Nebraska Press, Lincoln. But see also my books *The Ascent of Chiefs: Cahokia and Mississippian Politics in Native North America,* University of Alabama Press, Tuscaloosa (1994), *Ancient Cahokia and the Mississippians,* Cambridge University Press, Cambridge (2004), *North American Archaeology,* edited by T. R. Pauketat and D. D. Loren, Blackwell, Oxford (2005), and *Chiefdoms and Other Archaeological Delusions,* AltaMira Press, Walnut Canyon, California (2007).

2. David La Vere, *Looting Spiro Mounds: An American King Tut's Tomb,* University of Oklahoma Press, Norman (2007).

3. James A. Brown, *The Spiro Ceremonial Center: The Archaeology of Arkansas Valley Caddoan Culture in Eastern Oklahoma,* University of Michigan, Museum of Anthropology, Memoirs Number 29, Ann Arbor (1996).

4. For the latest views on Monte Albán, see Arthur A. Joyce's "Sacred Space and Social Relations in the Valley of Oaxaca," in *Mesoamerican Archaeology: Theory and Practice,* edited by J. A. Hendon and R. A. Joyce, Blackwell, Oxford (2004), pp. 192–216. See also Joyce Marcus and Kent Flannery's *Zapotec Civilization:*

How Urban Society Evolved in Mexico's Oaxaca Valley, Thames and Hudson, London (1996).

5. All dates in this book are CE (Common Era) or AD (anno Domini), unless noted as BCE (before the Common Era) or BC (before Christ).

6. James Mooney, *The Ghost-Dance Religion and Wounded Knee,* Dover Publications, New York (1973).

7. The classic example of a Cahokia-connected town in the north is Aztalan, near Madison, Wisconsin: see Robert A. Birmingham and Lynne G. Goldstein, *Aztalan: Mysteries of an Ancient Indian Town,* Wisconsin Historical Society Press, Madison, Wisconsin (2007). However, the best examples of Cahokians in the northlands are found near La Crosse: see Danielle Benden, "The Fisher Mounds Site Complex: Early Middle Mississippian Exploration in the Upper Mississippi Valley," *Minnesota Archaeologist* 63 (2004), pp. 17–24; Robert F. Boszhardt, "The Late Woodland and Middle Mississippian Component at the Iva Site, La Crosse County, Wisconsin, in the Driftless Area of the Upper Mississippi River Valley," *Minnesota Archaeologist* 63 (2004), pp. 60–85; and William Green and Roland L. Rodell, "The Mississippian Presence and Cahokia Interaction at Trempealeau, Wisconsin," *American Antiquity* 59 (1994), pp. 334–59.

CHAPTER 2: SUPERNOVA

1. See Timothy R. Pauketat and Susan M. Alt, "Mounds, Memory, and Contested Mississippian History," in *Archaeologies of Memory,* edited by R. M. Van Dyke and S. E. Alcock, Blackwell, Oxford (2003), pp. 151–79.

2. Eric Hobsbawm and Terrance Ranger, editors, *The Invention of Tradition,* Cambridge University Press, Cambridge (1983); Timothy R. Pauketat, editor, *The Archaeology of Traditions: Agency and History Before and After Columbus,* University Press of Florida, Gainesville (2001).

3. Simon Mitton, *The Crab Nebula,* Charles Scribner's Sons, New York (1978), and F. Richard Stephenson and David A. Green, *Historical Supernovae and Their Remnants,* Clarendon Press, Oxford (2002).

4. Carol M. Diaz-Granados and James R. Duncan, *The Petroglyphs and Pictographs of Missouri,* University of Alabama Press, Tuscaloosa (2000).

5. John Kantner, personal communication, December 2006. See also his book *Ancient Puebloan Southwest,* Cambridge University Press, Cambridge (2004), and the original tree-ring study by William J. Robinson, Bruce G. Harrill, and Richard L. Warren, *Tree-Ring Dates from New Mexico B: Chaco-Gobernador Area,* The Laboratory of Tree-Ring Research, University of Arizona, Tucson (1974).

CHAPTER 3: WALKING INTO CAHOKIA

1. These and more comparisons can be found in Norman Yoffee's *Myths of the Archaic State: Evolution of the Earliest Cities, States, and Civilizations,* Cambridge University Press, Cambridge (2005).
2. Of course, the Illini people had been in this part of Illinois for less than a century when this question was asked by the elder Clark. They had been pushed west from northern Ohio and Indiana under pressure from Iroquoian groups. James Alton James, *The Life of George Rogers Clark,* University of Chicago Press, Chicago (1928), p. 497.
3. Henry Marie Brackenridge, *Views of Louisiana* (originally published in 1814), Quadrangle Books, Chicago, (1962), pp. 187–89.
4. Ibid.
5. Ibid.
6. Ibid.

CHAPTER 4: THE ORIGINAL ROLLING STONES

1. The odors of one Arikara village proved too much for the intrepid Henry Marie Brackenridge, who had traveled west to see the frontier. "Rambled through the village," he notes, "which I found excessively filthy" and "swarming with dogs and children." "[V]illainous smells," Brackenridge states, "every where assailed me, [and] compelled me at length, to seek refuge in the open plain" (*Views of Louisiana,* originally published in 1814 [reprinted by Quadrangle Books, Chicago, 1962], p. 247).
2. See Stewart Culin, *Games of the North American Indians,* Volume 2, University of Nebraska Press, Lincoln (1992), and George Catlin, *Letters and Notes on the North American Indians,* JG Press, North Dighton, Massachusetts (1995).
3. Henry S. Halbert, "The Choctaw Achahpih (Chungkee) Game," *American Antiquarian* 10 (1888), pp. 283–84, cited by John R. Swanton, *Source Material for the Social and Ceremonial Life of the Choctaw Indians,* University of Alabama Press, Tuscaloosa (2001), p. 157.
4. James Adair, *The History of the American Indians* (originally published in 1775), edited by K. E. H. Braund, University of Alabama Press, Tuscaloosa, p. 401.
5. A Spanish priest in the Deep South saw a variant of the game in which the players and the town chief gathered at one end of the plaza, each player with a throwing pole and the chief holding the chunkey stone. Then the chief sent the disk "rolling with his whole strength," and the players "all at one time and without

order threw their staffs after the stone and at the same time started after them on the run." Although the priest was confused by the play, he thought that "he who ran fastest and arrived first took his staff and the stone and without stopping a moment returned to dart it at the place which they had left, and in the same manner the others took theirs and returned to dart them" (cited by John Swanton in *The Indians of the Southeastern United States,* Smithsonian Institution Press, Washington, D.C. [1979], p. 683).

6. Cited secondhand by Culin, *Games of the North American Indians,* Volume 2, pp. 486–87; see also Gregory A. Waselkov and Kathryn E. Holland Braund, *William Bartram on the Southeastern Indians,* University of Nebraska Press, Lincoln (1995), pp. 154–55.

7. Culin, *Games of the North American Indians,* Volume 2, pp. 485–88, 511–13. See also *The Journal of Rudolph Friederich Kurz,* University of Nebraska Press, Lincoln (1970).

8. Gregory H. Perino, "The Mississippian Component at the Schild Site (No. 4), Greene County, Illinois," in *Mississippian Site Archaeology in Illinois* 1, Illinois Archaeological Survey, Bulletin No. 8, Urbana, Illinois (1971), pp. 112–16.

9. James A. Brown, *The Spiro Ceremonial Center: The Archaeology of Arkansas Valley Caddoan Culture in Eastern Oklahoma,* University of Michigan, Museum of Anthropology, Memoirs Number 29, Ann Arbor (1996).

10. Thomas E. Emerson and Randall E. Hughes, "Figurines, Flint Clay Sourcing, the Ozark Highlands, and Cahokian Acquisition," *American Antiquity* 65 (2000), pp. 79–101; Thomas E. Emerson, Randall E. Hughes, Mary R. Hynes, and Sarah U. Wisseman, "Implications of Sourcing Cahokia-Style Flint Clay Figures in the American Bottom and the Upper Mississippi River Valley," *Midcontinental Journal of Archaeology* 27 (2002), pp. 309–38; and Thomas E. Emerson, Randall E. Hughes, Mary R. Hynes, and Sarah U. Wisseman, "The Sourcing and Interpretation of Cahokia-Style Figurines in the Trans-Mississippi South and Southeast," *American Antiquity* 68 (2003), pp. 287–313.

CHAPTER 5: GHOSTS OF ARCHAEOLOGISTS

1. Bilone W. Young and Melvin L. Fowler, *Cahokia: The Great Native American Metropolis,* University of Illinois Press, Urbana (2000).

2. Gary E. Moulton, editor, *The Definitive Journals of Lewis & Clark: From the Ohio to the Vermilion,* Volume 2, University of Nebraska Press, Lincoln (1986), pp. 153–54.

3. Young and Fowler, *Cahokia: The Great Native American Metropolis,* p. 85.

4. Patrick Munson, interview with the author, October 22, 2004.

5. Ibid.

6. Unpublished notes on file at the Illinois State Museum, Springfield, Illinois.

7. Ibid.

8. Alice B. Kehoe, *The Land of Prehistory: A Critical History of American Archaeology,* Routledge, London (1998).

9. Joyce Wike, interview with the author, October 15–16, 2000.

10. See Giuseppe Mastrolorenzo, Pier P. Petrone, Mario Pagano, Alberto Incoronato, Peter J. Baxter, Antonio Canzanella, and Luciano Fattore, "Herculaneum Victims of Vesuvius in AD 79," *Nature* 410 (2001), pp. 769–70.

11. Unpublished field notes on file at the University of Michigan Museum of Anthropology, Ann Arbor.

CHAPTER 6: DISCOVERY AT MOUND 72

1. At the time, Al Meyer was an art teacher at the same place, Belleville Township High School West, that had produced Gregory Perino years earlier (and, later, would produce myself and Brad Koldehoff).

2. See chapter 3, note 3.

3. Biloine Whiting Young and Melvin L. Fowler, *Cahokia: The Great Native American Metropolis,* University of Illinois Press, Urbana (2000), p. 123.

4. Ibid.

5. Jerome C. Rose, "Mortuary Data and Analysis," in *The Mound 72 Area: Dedicated and Sacred Space in Early Cahokia,* by M. Fowler, J. Rose, B. Vander Leest, and S. Ahler, Illinois State Museum, Reports of Investigations, No. 54, Springfield (1999), pp. 63–82.

6. Stephen Williams and Jeffrey P. Brain, *Excavations at the Lake George Site, Yazoo County, Mississippi, 1958–1960,* Papers of the Peabody Museum of Archaeology and Ethnology, Volume 74, Harvard University, Cambridge, Massachusetts (1983).

7. See Robert L. Hall's masterpiece, *An Archaeology of the Soul: North American Indian Belief and Ritual,* University of Illinois Press, Urbana (1997), and especially his paper "Sacrificed Foursomes and Green Corn Ceremonialism," in *Mounds, Modoc, and Mesoamerica: Papers in Honor of Melvin L. Fowler,* edited by S. R. Ahler, Illinois State Museum Scientific Papers, Volume 28, Springfield (2000), pp. 245–53. From a Mesoamerican vantage point, see Mary Miller and Karle Taube, *An Illustrated Dictionary of the Gods and Symbols of Ancient Mexico and the Maya,* Thames and Hudson, London (1993); Michel Graulich,

Myths of Ancient Mexico, University of Oklahoma Press, Norman (1997); and Kay Almere Read and Jason J. Gonzalez, *Mesoamerican Mythology: A Guide to the Gods, Heroes, Rituals, and Beliefs of Mexico and Central America,* Oxford University Press, Oxford (2000).

8. Paul Radin, *Winnebago Hero Cycles: A Study in Aboriginal Literature,* Waverly Press, Baltimore (1948), p. 129; see also Hall, *An Archaeology of the Soul,* pp. 4, 58; and Robert L. Hall, "The Cultural Background of Mississippian Symbolism," in *The Southeastern Ceremonial Complex,* edited by P. Galloway, University of Nebraska Press, Lincoln (1989), pp. 239–78.

9. F. Kent Reilly III and James F. Garber, *Ancient Objects and Sacred Realms: Interpretations of Mississippian Iconography,* University of Texas Press, Austin (2007).

CHAPTER 7: TWIN HEROES

1. See Robert A. Birmingham and Lynne G. Goldstein, *Aztalan: Mysteries of an Ancient Indian Town,* Wisconsin Historical Society Press, Madison (2007); Robert F. Boszhardt, "The Late Woodland and Middle Mississippian Component at the Iva Site, La Crosse County, Wisconsin, in the Driftless Area of the Upper Mississippi River Valley," *Minnesota Archaeologist* 63 (2004), pp. 60–85; and William Green and Roland L. Rodell, "The Mississippian Presence and Cahokia Interaction at Trempealeau, Wisconsin," *American Antiquity* 59 (1994), pp. 334–59.

2. Paul Radin, *The Winnebago Tribe,* University of Nebraska Press, Lincoln (1990). See also his *Winnebago Hero Cycles: A Study in Aboriginal Literature,* Waverly Press, Baltimore (1948).

3. Carol Diaz-Granados, "Marking Stone, Land, Body, and Spirit: Rock Art and Mississippian Iconography," in *Hero, Hawk and Open Hand: American Indian Art of the Ancient Midwest and South,* edited by R. Townsend, Yale University Press, New Haven, Connecticut (2004), pp. 139–49. See also Carol M. Diaz-Granados and James R. Duncan, *The Petroglyphs and Pictographs of Missouri,* University of Alabama Press, Tuscaloosa (2000).

4. Robert J. Salzer and Grace Rajnovich, *The Gottschall Rockshelter: An Archaeological Mystery,* Prairie Smoke Press, St. Paul, Minnesota (2000).

5. From the account of Jasper Blowsnake, published by Paul Radin in *Winnebago Hero Cycles,* p. 117.

6. This and other aspects of the Red Horn, Morning Star, and Long-Nosed God stories are discussed in Robert L. Hall's *An Archaeology of the Soul: North American Indian Belief and Ritual,* University of Illinois Press, Urbana (1997), p. 150.

7. John Witthoft, *Green Corn Ceremonialism in the Eastern Woodlands,* University of Michigan Press, Ann Arbor (1948).

8. Robert L. Hall, "Sacrificed Foursomes and Green Corn Ceremonialism," in *Mounds, Modoc, and Mesoamerica: Papers in Honor of Melvin L. Fowler,* edited by S. R. Ahler, Illinois State Museum Scientific Papers, Volume 28, Springfield (2000), pp. 245–53.

9. Paul Radin, Winnebago Hero Cycles: A Study in Aboriginal Literature. Indiana University Publications in Anthropology and Linguistics, supplement to *International Journal of American Linguistics* 14, No. 3 (1948), p. 45.

CHAPTER 8: AMERICAN INDIAN ROYALTY

1. Stephen Williams and John M. Goggin, "The Long Nosed God Mask in Eastern United States," *Missouri Archaeologist* 18 (1956), p. 21.

2. Anonymous newspaper account from 1870, cited by John E. Kelly in *The Archaeology of the East St. Louis Mound Center,* edited by T. R. Pauketat, Illinois Transportation Archaeological Research Program, Report 21, University of Illinois, Urbana (2005), p. 20.

3. Ibid.

4. Robert L. Hall, "Sacrificed Foursomes and Green Corn Ceremonialism," in *Mounds, Modoc, and Mesoamerica: Papers in Honor of Melvin L. Fowler,* edited by S. R. Ahler, Illinois State Museum Scientific Papers, Volume 28, Springfield (2000), pp. 245–53.

5. Robert L. Hall cites Father Sagard's observations in his *An Archaeology of the Soul: North American Indian Belief and Ritual,* University of Illinois Press, Urbana (1997), p. 35.

6. Unpublished notes on file at the University of Michigan, Museum of Anthropology, Ann Arbor. See also Timothy R. Pauketat, *Temples for Cahokia Lords: Preston Holder's 1955–1956 Excavations of Kunnemann Mound,* Museum of Anthropology, University of Michigan, Memoir No. 26, Ann Arbor (1993).

7. Based on the most discrete feasting zones (D2 and F), as reported by Timothy R. Pauketat, Lucretia S. Kelly, Gayle J. Fritz, Neal H. Lopinot, Scott Elias, and Eve Hargrave, "The Residues of Feasting and Public Ritual at Early Cahokia," *American Antiquity* 67 (2002), pp. 257–79. As an interesting aside, smoking tobacco, feasting, and religious ritual were often synonymous for American Indians connected in some way with Cahokia. Radin, in *The Winnebago Tribe* (University of Nebraska, Lincoln, 1990), writes that not only was tobacco given to the Ho-Chunk by the creator but feasting was described as "pouring tobacco."

8. Norman Yoffee, *Myths of the Archaic State: Evolution of the Earliest Cities, States, and Civilizations,* Cambridge University Press, Cambridge (2005).

9. Thomas E. Emerson, *Cahokia and the Archaeology of Power,* University of Alabama Press, Tuscaloosa (1997); Thomas E. Emerson and Douglas K. Jackson, *The BBB-Motor Site (11-Ms-595),* American Bottom Archaeology, FAI-270 Site Reports 6, University of Illinois Press, Urbana (1984); Douglas K. Jackson, Andrew C. Fortier, and Joyce A. Williams, *The Sponemann Site 2 (11-Ms-517): The Mississippian and Oneota Occupations,* American Bottom Archaeology, FAI-270 Site Reports 24, University of Illinois Press, Urbana (1992).

CHAPTER 9: DIGGING FOR THE GODDESS

1. As told to Susan M. Alt by an archaeologist who shall remain unidentified, November 2001.

2. Susan M. Alt, "Cahokian Change and the Authority of Tradition," in *The Archaeology of Traditions: Agency and History Before and After Columbus,* edited by T. R. Pauketat, University Press of Florida, Gainesville (2001), pp. 141–56; and Susan M. Alt, "Identities, Traditions, and Diversity in Cahokia's Uplands," *Midcontinental Journal of Archaeology* 27 (2002), pp. 217–36. See also Timothy R. Pauketat, "Resettled Farmers and the Making of a Mississippian Polity," *American Antiquity* 68 (2003), pp. 39–66.

3. Susan M. Alt, "Cultural Pluralism and Complexity: Analyzing a Cahokian Ritual Outpost," unpublished Ph.D. dissertation, Department of Anthropology, University of Illinois, Urbana-Champaign (2006).

4. Susan M. Alt, "Spindle Whorls and Fiber Production at Early Cahokian Settlements," *Southeastern Archaeology* 18 (1999), pp. 124–33.

5. Stephen Williams, "The Vacant Quarter and Other Late Events in the Lower Valley," in *Towns and Temples Along the Mississippi,* edited by D. H. Dye, University of Alabama Press, Tuscaloosa (1990), pp. 170–80.

6. Rinita A. Dalan, George R. Holley, William I. Woods, Harold W. Watters, Jr., and John A. Koepke, *Envisioning Cahokia: A Landscape Perspective,* Northern Illinois University Press, DeKalb (2003).

7. Eric Powell, "Cold Hard Cache," *Archaeology* 54, No. 6, news brief (2001): http://www.archaeology.org/0111/newsbriefs/cache.html.

8. Stanley H. Ambrose, Jane Buikstra, and Harold W. Krueger, "Status and Gender Differences in Diet at Mound 72, Cahokia, Revealed by Isotopic Analysis of Bone," *Journal of Anthropological Archaeology* 22 (2003), pp. 217–26.

CHAPTER 10: WRESTLING WITH THE GODS

1. Philip Phillips, James A. Ford, and James B. Griffin, *Archaeological Survey in the Lower Mississippi Alluvial Valley, 1940–1947,* Papers of the Peabody Museum of Archaeology and Ethnology, Volume 25, Harvard University, Cambridge, Massachusetts (1951).

2. Antonio J. Waring and Preston Holder, "A Prehistoric Ceremonial Complex in the Southeastern United States," *American Anthropologist* 47 (1945), pp. 1–34.

3. James Brown, "6000 Years of Mound Building," *Cambridge Archaeological Journal* 15 (2005), pp. 113–15.

4. Robert L. Hall, *An Archaeology of the Soul: North American Indian Belief and Ritual,* University of Illinois Press, Urbana (1997), p. 162.

5. Nancy M. White, ed., *Gulf Coast Archaeology: The Southeastern United States and Mexico,* University Press of Florida, Gainesville (2005).

6. Alice B. Kehoe, "Wind Jewels and Paddling Gods: The Mississippian Southeast in the Postclassic Mesoamerican World," in *Gulf Coast Archaeology: The Southeastern United States and Mexico,* edited by N. M. White, University Press of Florida, Gainesville (2005), pp. 260–80.

7. Alex W. Barker, Craig E. Skinner, M. Steven Shackley, Michael D. Glascock, and J. Daniel Rogers, "Mesoamerican Origin for an Obsidian Scraper from the Precolumbian Southeastern United States," *American Antiquity* 67 (2002), pp. 103–8.

8. Hall, *An Archaeology of the Soul,* p. 166.

9. Ibid., pp. 162–63.

10. Mary Miller and Karle Taube, *An Illustrated Dictionary of the Gods and Symbols of Ancient Mexico and the Maya,* Thames and Hudson, London (1993), p. 88.

11. Stephen Williams and John M. Goggin, "The Long Nosed God Mask in Eastern United States," *Missouri Archaeologist* 18 (1956).

12. One story placed them in a closet at Washington University in St. Louis before Preston Holder's arrival there. That story ends with a tragedy: To Holder's chagrin, the university community was narrowly focused on Old World archaeology, and at some point, one of the professors or perhaps a janitor cleaned out the closet and discarded the undervalued North American artifacts.

13. Ibid. See also Robert Hall, "Cahokia Identity and Interaction Models of Cahokia Mississippian," in *Cahokia and the Hinterlands: Middle Mississippian Cultures of the Midwest,* edited by T. E. Emerson and R. B. Lewis, University of Illinois Press, Urbana (1991), pp. 3–34; and James R. Duncan and Carol Diaz-Granados, "Of Masks and Myths," *Midcontinental Journal of Archaeology* 25 (2000), pp. 1–26.

14. Hall, "Cahokia Identity"; and Guy E. Gibbon, "A Model of Mississippian Development and Its Implications for the Red Wing Area," in *Aspects of Upper Great Lakes Anthropology,* edited by E. Johnson, Minnesota Prehistoric Archaeology Series 11 (1974), pp. 129–37.

15. Robert L. Hall, "The Cultural Background of Mississippian Symbolism," in *The Southeastern Ceremonial Complex: Artifacts and Analysis,* edited by P. Galloway, University of Nebraska Press, Lincoln (1989), pp. 239–78.

16. The circular earspools of other noblemen and women in the ridgetop mounds at Cahokia or found in various parts of Mesoamerica might have been intended at one point to represent the goggle eyes of the great creator and earth god or his heirs, the twins.

17. Mary W. Helms, *Ulysses' Sail: An Ethnographic Odyssey of Power, Knowledge, and Geographical Distance,* Princeton University Press, Princeton, New Jersey (1988).

CHAPTER 11: TREASURE MAPS OF THE PAST

1. Gary E. Moulton, *The Definitive Journals of Lewis & Clark: From the Ohio to the Vermillion,* Volume 2, University of Nebraska Press, Lincoln (1986), pp. 102–3.

2. F. Terry Norris and Timothy R. Pauketat, "A Pre-Columbian Map of the Mississippi?" *Southeastern Archaeology* 27 (2008), pp. 78–92.

3. Mark Warhus, *Another America: Native American Maps and the History of Our Land,* St. Martin's Press, New York (1997); Garrick Mallery, *Picture Writing of the American Indians,* Tenth Annual Report of the Bureau of Ethnology, Smithsonian Institution, Government Printing Office, Washington, D.C. (1893); Robert J. Salzer and Grace Rajnovich, *The Gottschall Rockshelter: An Archaeological Mystery,* Prairie Smoke Press, St. Paul, Minnesota (2000).

4. Richard Bradley, *The Significance of Monuments: On the Shaping of Human Experience in Neolithic and Bronze Age Europe,* Routledge, London (1998); Chris Gosden and G. Lock, "Prehistoric Histories," in *World Archaeology* 30 (1998), pp. 2–12.

5. Timothy P. McCleary, *The Stars We Know: Crow Indian Astronomy and Lifeways,* Waveland Press, Prospect Heights, Illinois (1997), p. 42.

6. Richard F. Townsend, editor, *Hero, Hawk, and Open Hand: American Indian Art of the Ancient Midwest and South,* Art Institute of Chicago and Yale University Press, New Haven, Connecticut (2004); V. James Knight, Jr., James A. Brown, and George E. Lankford, "On the Subject Matter of Southeastern Ceremonial Complex Art," *Southeastern Archaeology* 20 (2001), pp. 129–41.

7. Stephen H. Lekson, *Chaco Meridian: Centers of Political Power in the Ancient*

Southwest, AltaMira Press, Walnut Canyon, California (1999); Stephen H. Lekson and Catherine M. Cameron, "The Abandonment of Chaco Canyon, the Mesa Verde Migrations, and the Reorganization of the Pueblo World," *Journal of Anthropological Archaeology* 14 (1995), pp. 184–202.

CHAPTER 12: HIGH PLAINS DRIFTING

1. Preston Holder, *The Hoe and the Horse on the Plains,* University of Nebraska Press, Lincoln (1970).
2. P. Willey and Thomas E. Emerson, "The Osteology and Archaeology of the Crow Creek Massacre," *Plains Anthropologist* 38 (1990), pp. 227–69.
3. Ibid., see chapter 10, note 13.
4. Alice Fletcher, *Hako,* University of Nebraska Press, Lincoln (1996), pp. 301–2.

INDEX

Adair, James, 41–43, 47, 50
adoption ceremonies, 146
agriculture, *see* farmers and
    agriculture
Algonkian tribes, 125
Alt, Susan, 122, 127, 130, 131
Ambrose, Stan, 133
American Woodhenge, 62–64, 70, 112,
    114, 161–63
Anderson, Jim, 72
archaeologists, 4–6, 51–68, 169
    evolutionary theories and, 105–6
    male bias among, 113
    Native American art as viewed by,
        157–58
    women's role in Cahokia
        reevaluated by, 114–18
Archaeology, 130
Arikara, 37, 163–65
arrows, 78, 82–83, 91, 153

axe heads, 130–32, 153
Aztalan site, 145

Bareis, Charles, 58, 63, 71, 79, 106,
    108, 114, 120, 128, 154, 164
Bartram, William, 41
BBB-Motor site, 114–16
beaded-cape burials, 72–74, 77–79,
    81–83, 85, 101, 112
Big Horn Medicine Wheel, 161–62
Big Mound, 26, 27, 28, 101–2, 143–44,
    146
bison robe, 158
Blowsnake, Jasper, 88
Boas, Franz, 52, 88
Booth, Don, 129
bows, 44–45
Brackenridge, Henry Marie, 27–29,
    35, 56, 61, 71, 129
Brown, James, 138

Buikstra, Jane, 133
burials, 65–68, 72, 91, 99–106
  beaded-cape, 72–74, 77–79, 81–83,
    85, 101, 112
  at Mound 72, 69–70, 73–84, 91, 93,
    100–103, 110, 112, 128,
    132–33
  sacrificial, 66, 80, 93, 100, 102–3,
    110, 112–13, 128, 131–34, 165,
    169

Caddoan speakers, 37, 38, 94, 116, 124,
  125, 137, 145, 162, 163
Cahokia:
  absence from narratives, 159–60
  "big bang" at, 4, 9, 10, 15, 46, 97–98,
    106, 147
  center of, 34–35, 126–27
  descendants of inhabitants, 37–38,
    124–25, 164, 168–69
  end of, 164, 168
  New, 21–24
  Old, 15–16, 19–21, 23, 61–62, 127
  population of, 2, 14, 26, 63–64, 126
  residential neighborhoods of,
    59–60, 70, 107
  size of, 26–27
  topographical map made of,
    70–72
  walking into, 29–35
Cahokia Mounds State Historic Site,
  3, 25, 154, 162
Calumet, 166
Casa Rinconada, 21
Catlin, George, 39, 40, 50, 95, 125
Cayuga, 95
Cemetery Mound, 28, 102, 129

Chac, 12, 142, 147
Chaco Canyon, 12–13, 20–21, 156,
  159
Champlain, Samuel de, 156
Cherokee, 95, 96
Chickasaw, 156
Chiwere language, 38
Choctaw, 47, 156
chunkey, 35, 36, 39–50, 111–13, 122,
  162, 165, 168
  burials and, 81, 82, 83
  stones, 41–47, 49, 81, 82, 83, 152,
    153, 165–66
Chunkey Player pipe, 48, 49
Clark, George Rogers, 27
Clark, William, 27, 36, 37, 38, 40, 57,
  125, 152, 168
Copán, 159
corn (maize), 8, 13, 18, 45, 133–34,
  136, 138, 141, 170
Corn Mother, 94–96, 103, 117, 132,
  133, 141, 149, 169
cosmos, 7, 43, 128
council houses, 14–15, 61, 130
Coyolxauhqui, 96
creation, 1, 43, 94, 96, 111, 132, 141,
  148
Crow, 37, 38, 94, 149, 162
Crow Creek massacre, 164–65, 167
crystals, 19, 78, 83, 91, 101

daggers, 7, 142–43, 147, 148
Dakota, 37, 47
Dalan, Rinita, 126–27
Danzantes, 5–6, 117
Depression, Great, 53
De Soto, Hernando, 124, 125

Dhegiha speakers, 38, 124, 158, 162
Diaz-Granados, Carol, 145–46
Ducoign, Chief, 27
Duncan, Jim, 145–46

ear ornaments, 7, 66, 90, 97, 143–47,
    148, 169, 170
East St. Louis, 3, 26–28, 100–104, 126,
    129–30
effigy mounds, 17, 86, 89
Eisenhower, Dwight D., 56, 61
Emerson, Thomas, 47–49, 106, 110,
    114–17, 130, 164–65
esoteric knowledge, 148–49
Europeans, 11, 17, 36, 39–40, 124,
    168–69
Evening Star, 1, 2, 8, 94, 117, 141,
    170
evolutionary theories, 105–6
expansion, U.S., 36–37, 39, 168–69
explorers, 36–37, 39, 41, 125
    Lewis and Clark, 27, 36, 37, 38, 40,
        57, 125, 152

farmers and agriculture, 2, 14, 18, 33,
    106, 118, 119–23, 125–26, 134–35,
    164, 169
    axe head burials and, 130–32
    corn (maize) and, 8, 13, 18, 45,
        133–34, 136, 138, 141, 170
festivals, 14, 109–12, 128
Finiels, Nicolas de, 151
Finney, Fred, 129
Fletcher, Alice, 166
flint, 7, 142–43
Ford, Jim, 53
Fortier, Andrew, 114–15, 129

Fowler, Melvin, 55–60, 64, 68, 69–74,
    79, 106, 117, 152
Friedel, David, 158

Gahagan site, 145
gambling, 42
garbage pits, 15, 16, 19, 121
    sub-Mound 51, 108–9, 112, 128
Gibbon, Guy, 166
goddesses, 1
    Corn Mother, 94–96, 103, 117, 132,
        133, 141, 149, 169
    sculptures of, 115–17
gods, 1, 8, 13, 14, 44, 146–47, 159
    long-nosed, 90, 96, 144–49, 169
Goggin, John, 144–45
Gottschall Rockshelter, 85–91, 97, 113,
    116, 142
government, 7–8, 15, 16, 110–11
Grand Plaza, 23, 25, 28, 34–35, 53,
    108, 126–28
Grange Terre, Le, 27
Great Houses, 13, 20–21, 159
Great Mortuary, 4–5
Great Plains, 37–38
Griffin, James B., 59–60, 66, 119–20,
    136, 137, 147
Grossmann site, 130

Hako, 166
Hall, Robert, 62, 63, 88, 96, 103, 106,
    120, 138–42, 146, 147, 159, 161,
    164, 166
    Wittry and, 163
Halliday site, 119–22, 132, 134
Harn, Alan, 60
Helms, Mary, 148

hero-twin stories, 81–82, 92–98, 101, 104, 117, 142, 147, 148, 162, 169

He-who-wears-human-heads-as-earrings (Red Horn), 88, 90–98, 117, 142, 143–44, 146, 148

Hidatsa, 37, 38, 40, 94–95, 104, 116, 142, 156

highways, interstate, 56–59, 61, 63, 107, 114, 164

Hiwassee Island, 53

Ho-Chunk (Winnebago), 38, 88, 89, 156
   myths of, 82, 88, 91–94, 96, 97, 101, 116, 142, 144, 148

Holder, Preston, 51–56, 59, 64–68, 72, 100, 103, 106–8, 116, 117, 136–37, 163, 164

Holley, George, 126–27

Honga, 104, 141

hoop-and-pole game, 39, 44, 45

houses, 2, 13–15, 21–22, 30–31, 106–7, 120–21, 153

Hun Hunahpu, 142

Hurley, William, 60

Illinois, 25

Illinois State Museum, 59, 60

impersonators, 94–95, 104–5, 110, 117, 141, 159, 162

Iowa Indians, 88, 89, 93, 94, 101, 116, 144

Irene, 53

Iroquois, 95, 111

Jackson, Douglas, 114–15

Japan, 53

Jefferson, Thomas, 27, 29, 168

Junkyard Mound, 64–68, 100, 103–4, 107, 112, 128, 134, 163

Kansa, 38, 158

Kansas City Star, 4

Kehoe, Alice, 96, 140, 143, 148

Kelly, John, 102, 106, 129

"Killing the Gods and Burning the Thrones" (Friedel), 158

knives, 7, 142–43, 147, 148

Koldehoff, Brad, 146

Kruchten, Jeff, 127, 130

Kunnemann Mound, 107, 108, 163

Kurz, Rudolph, 39, 42

Lake George, 80

Lakota, 164, 169

Lekson, Steve, 159

Lewis, Meriwether, 27, 36, 37, 38, 40, 57, 125, 152

lineages, 67

locatives, 83, 91

Long Arm, 142

Long-Nosed Gods, 90, 96, 147–49
   ear ornaments, 144–47, 169

Louisiana, 17, 138–40, 145

Louisiana Purchase, 168

Macon Plateau, 53

maize (corn), 8, 13, 18, 45, 133–34, 136, 138, 141, 170

male/female duality, 43, 94, 97, 111

Mandan, 37, 38, 40, 47, 94–95, 104, 149

maps, 156–57
   rock-art, 8, 152–57, 165, 166

massacre at Crow Creek, 164–65, 167

matrilineal societies, 67

Mead, Margaret, 4

Mehrer, Mark, 106

Mesoamerica, 2, 7, 12, 70, 80, 95–98, 103, 135, 136–50, 169

Mexico, 3, 8, 9, 12, 80, 96, 136–37, 139–41, 146–49, 158–59

Meyer, Albert, 69, 70, 73–75, 101

mica crystals, 78, 83, 91, 101

migrations, 37–38, 122–25, 158, 168, 169

military actions, 165–68

Milky Way, 13, 20

Miller, Mary, 142

Milner, George, 106

Mimbres valley, 12, 20

Mississippian culture, 8, 23–24, 45, 136–50, 169

Mississippi River, 9, 17, 26, 27, 151–54, 162

bluffs of, 31–32

Mississippi River valley, 6, 13, 17–18, 23

Missouri River, 37, 168

Mitchell site, 57, 100, 101, 104

Monks Mound, 26, 29, 34–35, 54, 56, 59, 61, 71, 72, 108, 126, 158, 163

Monte Albán, 5–6, 12, 26, 117

Mooney, James, 40

Moorehead, Warren King, 54–56, 72, 100, 117

Morning Star, 1, 2, 8, 94, 97, 101, 103, 113, 117, 134, 141, 142, 170

mortuary spectacles, 104–5, 110, 111, 128, 129, 169

Mound Builders, 3, 17, 60

mounds (pyramids), 2–3, 9, 15–19, 22–24, 27–29, 34, 37, 54, 59, 70, 71, 96, 114, 126

Big Mound, 26, 27, 28, 101–2, 143–44, 146

Cemetery Mound, 28, 102, 129

destruction and erosion of, 2–3, 25, 26, 53, 58, 103

effigy, 17, 86, 89

Junkyard Mound, 64–68, 100, 102–4, 107, 112, 128, 134, 163

Kunnemann Mound, 107, 108, 163

Mesoamerican influence and, 137–38, 140

Monks Mound, 26, 29, 34–35, 54, 56, 59, 61, 71, 72, 108, 126, 158, 163

Mound 51, 58, 108

Mound 72, 55, 64, 69–84, 85, 91, 93, 100–103, 110, 112, 119, 128, 132–33, 152–53

Powell Mound, 28, 58, 100, 103–4

Rattlesnake Mound, 54, 100

ridgetop, 27–28, 99–105, 106, 111, 128, 132, 165, 169

sub-Mound 51 borrow pit, 108–9, 112, 128

as works in progress, 107–8

Munson, Patrick, 60, 61

Muskogee, 47, 95

myths, *see* religion and myth

Natchez, 80, 94, 95, 116

National Science Foundation (NSF), 49, 57, 58, 70

New Cahokia, 21–24

New Deal programs, 52–53, 59, 136

New Mexico, 12–13
Norris, Terry, 151–57, 165, 166
North Star, 82
nose cutting, 146

O'Brien, Patricia, 154–55
obsidian, 139, 140–41
Ojibwa, 156
Old Cahokia, 15–16, 19–21, 23, 61–62, 127
Omaha Indians, 13, 37, 38, 40, 104, 112, 158
Osage, 37, 38, 40, 96, 104, 124, 158, 168–69

Pawnee, 37–38, 40, 47, 80, 103, 113, 124, 132, 134, 141, 149, 159, 169
peacemaking envoys, 166
Peñasco Blanco, 20–21
Perino, Gregory, 45, 46, 48, 54–55, 145, 165
Peru, 8, 12
Picture Cave, 89–91, 113, 116, 142, 146
pipes, 48–49, 120, 124, 145, 162
    Chunkey Player, 48, 49
plazas, 2, 34, 41, 59, 70, 96, 114, 140
    chunkey played in, 41, 44
    Grand Plaza, 23, 25, 28, 34–35, 53, 108, 126–28
Plains Indians, 13, 37–38
politics, 1–2, 4, 43, 128, 130, 166
    killings and, 67–68
Ponca, 37, 38, 158
Popul Vuh, 96–97, 142
Portable Infrared Mineral Analyzer (PIMA), 49, 116

Porter, James, 57–58, 62, 63, 106, 114–15, 137, 154, 164
posts, 7, 13, 22, 31, 34, 41, 72, 111
    American Woodhenge, 62–64, 70, 112, 114, 161–63
    chunkey and, 41, 44
pottery, 9, 15, 16, 19, 20, 121–22
Poverty Point, 17
Powell Mound, 28, 58, 100, 103–4
Pueblo Bonito, 21
pyramids, *see* mounds

Quapaw, 38, 124, 158
Quetzalcoatl, 96, 147
Quiche Maya, 96
Quimby, George, 53

Radin, Paul, 88, 90, 92–93, 97
Ramey knives, 143, 148
Ramey state, 154
Rattlesnake Mound, 54, 100
Red Horn (He-who-wears-human-heads-as-earrings), 88, 90–98, 117, 142, 143–44, 146, 148
Red Horn panel, 87–90, 113
red-stone carvings, 106, 116–17
reincarnation rites, 104–5
religion and myth, 1, 7–8, 9, 110
    chunkey and, 43–44
    and control of esoteric knowledge, 148–49
    Corn Mother in, 94–96, 103, 117, 132, 133, 141, 149, 169
    creation in, 43, 94, 96, 111, 132, 141, 148
    festivals and, 14, 109–12, 128
    goddesses, 1, 115–17

gods, 1, 8, 13, 14, 44, 146–47, 159
　Ho-Chunk, 82, 88, 91–94, 96, 97,
　　101, 116, 142, 144, 148
　impersonators and, 94–95, 104–5,
　　110, 117, 141, 159, 162
　Long-Nosed God in, 90, 96,
　　144–49, 169
　rock art and, 155, 157
　twin-hero stories in, 81–82, 92–98,
　　101, 104, 117, 142, 147, 148, 162,
　　169
　World Center Shrines and,
　　161–62
replacement hypothesis, 110
ridgetop mounds, 27–28, 99–105, 106,
　　111, 128, 132, 165, 169
rock art, 20–21
　Gottschall Rockshelter, 85–91, 97,
　　113, 116, 142
　maps, 8, 152–57, 165, 166
　Picture Cave, 89–91, 113, 116, 142,
　　146
Roosevelt, Franklin D., 52–53, 136
Rose, Jerome, 74–77, 132–33

sacrifice, human, 7, 66, 80, 93, 100,
　　102–3, 110, 112–13, 128, 131–34,
　　141, 165, 169
Sagard, Gabriel, 104–5
Ste. Genevieve, 153
St. Louis, 2–3, 26–29, 36, 37, 51–52,
　　56, 100, 101, 104, 159
Salzer, Robert, 60, 86–90, 97
sculptures, 115–17
sedentary lifestyle, 45
7 Macaw, 142
Shiloh, 116

Siouan speakers, 38, 47, 93–94, 97, 104,
　　124, 125, 162, 165
Smith, Harriet, 53, 54, 71
Spain, 169
Spiro, 4–5, 37, 47, 48, 53, 116, 117, 137,
　　141, 146, 167
Sponemann site, 114–16
stars, 2, 8, 13, 82
　Evening, 1, 2, 8, 94, 117, 141, 170
　Morning, 1, 2, 8, 94, 97, 101, 103,
　　113, 117, 134, 141, 142, 170
　North, 82
　supernova, 20–21, 23–24, 111, 149,
　　156, 169
statuettes, 115–17, 167
stickball, 39–40, 42, 92, 168
sub-Mound 51 borrow pit, 108–9, 112,
　　128
Sun Dance, 162
supernova, 20–21, 23–24, 111, 149,
　　156, 169

Taube, Karle, 142
Tenochtitlán, 96
Teotihuacán, 12, 23, 159
theatrical spectacles, 104–5, 110, 111,
　　112, 128, 129, 162, 169
Thebes Gap, 123, 125, 151–55, 157,
　　166, 167
thunderbirds, 44, 94, 97, 101
Thunderers, 95, 101, 169
Tikal, 159
time, perception of, 156–58
Tlaloc, 12, 142, 147, 159
Toltec Mounds, 18–19
Toltec period, 12, 147–48
traders, 137

Troyville site, 140
Tula, 12, 21, 147
twin-hero stories, 81–82, 92–98,
    101, 104, 117, 142, 147, 148, 162,
    169

Vacant Quarter, 124
Valley of Oaxaca, 5–6
Varney pottery, 122
Venus, 96
    as Evening Star, 1, 2, 8, 94, 117, 141,
        170
    as Morning Star, 1, 2, 8, 94, 97,
        101, 103, 113, 117, 134, 141,
        142, 170

warfare, 165–68
Waring, Antonio, 136–37
water travel, 139
weapons, 167–68
    bows, 44–45
weaving, 121, 122–23
White, Nancy, 139
White Town, 159
Wichita, 149

Wike, Joyce, 51–52, 55, 56, 64–66, 68,
    72, 100, 103, 117, 163
Willey, Gordon, 52–53
Williams, Stephen, 124, 144–45
Wilson, Carrie, 158, 159
Winnebago, *see* Ho-Chunk
Wisconsin, 9, 86
Witthoft, John, 95
Wittry, Warren, 59–63, 70, 72, 79, 87,
    102, 106, 110, 113–14, 116, 162–64
    Hall and, 163
women, 114–18
    sacrificing of, 66, 100, 102, 110,
        112–13, 131–34, 169
Woodhenge, 62–64, 70, 112, 114,
    161–63
Woodland Indians, 13
Works Progress Administration
    (WPA), 53, 136
World Center Shrines, 161–62

Xipe Totec, 141
Xolotl, 96, 147

Yax-Kuk-Mo, 159